What people are saying about …

THE JOY OF LETTING GO

"Our hearts are always connected to our children, whether they are four or forty. In these fifty-two devotions, Vicki Caruana beautifully shows us that cutting the apron strings doesn't mean cutting the heart strings. This journey of letting go can be life-giving—for you and your children."

Jill Savage, founder of Hearts at Home
and author of *No More Perfect Kids*

"Vicki lovingly mixes her sense of humor, wisdom, and insights together in such a way that I know my friends will love this devotional as much as I do. Even though my own children are forty, thirty-eight, and thirty-seven, and I have a grandson in the Air Force, the challenge to find joy in the letting go remains. This devotional helps moms of all ages do just that. I'll be picking up multiple copies as gifts."

Francine Rivers, author of *Redeeming Love*

"Wisdom and grace are beautifully woven together in the pages of Vicki Caruana's book *The Joy of Letting Go*. Emptying the nest is a season, not an event, and Vicki offers powerful insight on how to walk through it without clipping our young birds' wings, even as she validates the angst moms feel. The book is designed in fifty-two short chapters, perfect for bite-sized daily readings—but I read the book in two sittings during a particularly trying week in my own letting-go process. I came away much more peaceful, standing in my decision to allow them to increase even as my role decreases."

Paula Moldenhauer, author of the
Soul Scents devotional series

"As a former educator and academic advisor, I wish I'd had this book to recommend to the parents of my high school seniors. It is much more than an empty-nest book—it is fifty-two counseling sessions to coach parents through the emotional and tangible challenges of launching their children. Bless your friends and family with this book—and then get one for yourself. It will be a dear companion as your child gets ready to head out on his or her own."

Janet Holm McHenry, author of twenty books
and college coach at SeniorYear101.com

"We raise our children so that they will be ready to leave us when the time comes. But when the time comes, it's not as easy as it sounds. In these short, pithy gems of wisdom, Vicki Caruana offers guidance and advice drawn from her experience as both a mother and an educator. Priceless."

Jennifer Kennedy Dean, executive director of The Praying Life Foundation and author of *Live a Praying Life* and numerous books and Bible studies

"Vicki Caruana is a master educator, skilled author, and wise mother, and she shares these gifts with us, showing us how to masterfully, skillfully, and wisely let our teens go. Her words paint pictures that linger, instruct, inspire, and illustrate how, and more important, why, to love our kids with a tender release. Practical and poignant. A must-read for moms."

Lindsey O'Connor, journalist, radio producer, and author of *The Long Awakening: A Memoir*

"Winsome stories coupled with experience and tried, tested, and proven perspective in the parenting marathon of life. Here you'll discover hard-won insights with just the right amount of humor as you make your way through its pages."

Julie Patrick-Barnhill, international
speaker and author of *She's Gonna Blow!*

"Part memoir, part inspiration, and thoroughly generous and kind. Vicki Caruana's friendly hand and spiritual touch will help parents who are reluctant to wave good-bye when much-loved children take wing."

Rachel Simon, *New York Times* bestselling
author of *The Story of Beautiful Girl*
and *Riding the Bus with My Sister*

THE JOY OF LETTING GO

*Releasing Your Teen into
Real Life in the Big World*

VICKI CARUANA

transforming lives together

THE JOY OF LETTING GO
Published by David C Cook
4050 Lee Vance Drive
Colorado Springs, CO 80918 U.S.A.

David C Cook U.K., Kingsway Communications
Eastbourne, East Sussex BN23 6NT, England

The graphic circle C logo is a registered trademark of David C Cook.

Details in some stories have been changed to protect
the identities of the persons involved.

Bible credits are listed at the back of this book.

LCCN 2016959751
ISBN 978-0-7814-1467-8
eISBN 978-1-4347-1053-6

Published in association with the Books & Such Literary
Management, 52 Mission Circle, Suite 122, PMB 170, Santa
Rosa, CA 95409-5370, www.booksandsuch.com.

The Team: Alice Crider, Nick Lee, Abby DeBenedittis,
Kayla Fenstermaker, Susan Murdock
Cover Design: Amy Konyndyk
Cover Photo: Getty Images

Printed in the United States of America

First Edition 2017

1 2 3 4 5 6 7 8 9 10

011217

To our sons, Christopher and
Charles, of whom I am proud
and for whom I am grateful

CONTENTS

ACKNOWLEDGMENTS

Each time I've written a book, a host of people have held me up—just as Aaron and Hur held up Moses's hands to ensure the victory of the Israelites. This book came at a time when so much was up in the air and my footing was unsure. My husband, Chip, is the rock I rested on when I became weary. His support of this call on my life has made me sturdy in my answer to it. Allowing me to use "our" stories freed me to be transparent in my writing. My agent, Rachelle Gardner, went ahead of me to prepare the way for this book. We had this vision together, and I'm grateful that she kept it moving until fruition. To my editor, Alice Crider, and the many fabulous folks at David

C Cook—from Darren Terpstra in marketing to Amy Konyndyk, who designed this beautiful cover—I felt we were all working toward the same promise.

I would also like to acknowledge the college where I teach as a professor of education. My colleagues at Mount Saint Mary College have supported my writing and the message I offer as a part of their mission. They actively make room for my work as desirable scholarship and find ways to celebrate it in the community.

Finally, I am thankful to our grown children, Christopher and Charles Caruana, who permitted the use of the stories from their lives for the sake of the readers. They approved each story before it was submitted to this book. I'm honored to be their mother.

INTRODUCTION

The prospect of an empty nest is supposed to be a good thing, right? Yet many moms are doing everything they can to delay it. We're holding on to our children for dear life, as if their growing up is our death. It is an ending of sorts—an ending to the life we've led for eighteen or more years. We have been involved, engaged, and intertwined in their education, their well-being, their extracurricular activities, even their friendships. We orchestrated much of it, and now we find ourselves a leader without a band.

Helping our kids learn to fend for themselves is not something we parents have spent much time agonizing over. We focused instead on stranger danger. We drove them to school rather than risk them walking or riding the dreaded bus. We spent most of our time creating just the right nurturing environment. No wonder so many of them never move out!

We've held on so tightly from the day we brought them home from the hospital in their state-of-the-art, ultrasafe car seat. We made sure they didn't get on a tricycle without a helmet. We got them fingerprint IDs from the sheriff's office when they were toddlers. We made sure they went to the right preschool and the right church and played with the right friends. We homeschooled, worked from home, and attended every soccer game, piano recital, and ballet lesson.

We drove the car of their lives with white knuckles— and now it's time to let go.

Not an easy thing to do, but oh so necessary. Not just for us, but for them. Our kids deserve a chance at their own lives, making their own choices and their own mistakes and taking their own bows.

We want the best for our children. We want them to have every advantage and to rise above mediocrity so they can soar to new heights. We want them to be successful, have a positive self-image, and enjoy their lives. We do everything we can to set them up to succeed—but at some point, we have to stop.

Letting go is a good thing. Letting go without warning, without preparation, and without awareness is not. How can we learn little by little to let go of our kids in ways that lead them to live their own lives and let us feel good about the hand we had in doing that? The longer you wait, the harder it is—on both of you. Letting go is a process, one that began the day they joined your family. You've already been letting go, but you may not be aware of it. *The Joy of Letting Go* shines a light on all the times you have loosened your grip—and encourages you to continue to let go in a safe and life-giving way.

Day 1

DEGREES OF SEPARATION

There are only two lasting bequests we can hope to give our children. One ... is roots, the other, wings.

Hodding Carter, *Where Main Street Meets the River*

The six-degrees-of-separation concept posits that any two people on earth are only six or fewer acquaintance links apart. At this point in my parenting journey, I thought there would never be more than one degree of separation between me and my children. After all, I can text them whenever I want. I can and should be able to get to them in the blink of an eye or by a tap on my smartphone. Yet the text I sent my younger son two days ago remains unanswered. He's busy. He's working. He's helping his older brother and his wife move. He's living his life—apart from me.

My mother always said, "Be careful what you wish for," and she was right. I wished for my children to be able to live lives that mattered, to be able to take care of themselves and others—to be independent. And they are. They live two thousand miles away from me, and I have to remember— I'm the one who moved!

But this independence thing may not be all it's cracked up to be. Don't get me wrong. I'm grateful that at this point we are no longer supporting our children financially. That, my friends, is an accomplishment worth celebrating. Sometimes, though, it's other types of support I miss. Where there was fellowship, emotional caretaking, and spiritual navigation, there's now a void. And the fact that I now have to watch *The Walking Dead* alone doesn't help.

When I think back to how this state of independence came to be, I see it didn't just happen. My husband, Chip, and I planned it. We put this in motion when we encouraged our firstborn to wait ten more minutes before we picked him up out of his crib and he slept through the night. I guess it probably happened even sooner than that. After all, we did cut the umbilical cord after birth. The first degree of separation between mother and child is natural and life-giving.

Be careful what you wish for? Yes, definitely, because it certainly might come true. For example, we want our child to sleep through the night, so we encourage him to do so, and then he doesn't need us to sleep through the night. He is able to sleep through the night because we wanted him to. See how that works? It's important to remember that you are still connected even if it takes a child three days to answer his mother's text.

THOUGHT POKE

Think back to a time when you purposely encouraged separation between yourself and your child. Can you see how that decision has affected your life? Remember that even in separation, God's promises prevail.

Peter replied, "Repent and be baptized, every one of you, in the name of Jesus Christ for the forgiveness of your sins. And you will receive the gift of the Holy Spirit. The promise is for you and your children and for all who are far off—for all whom the Lord our God will call." (Acts 2:38–39)

DO I STAY OR
DO I GO?

Don't cry because it's over. Smile because it happened.

Often attributed to Dr. Seuss

The image is still so strong. Every weekday for months, my five-year-old baby boy stood at the window of his pre-school with both hands on the glass, crying for me to stay. I couldn't. I had to go to work—as a teacher I had about thirty more children waiting for me to show up. I endured the daily exercise of letting go that school year in the most excruciating way. In my mind I see the palm prints of his small hands on the glass moments after his teacher enticed him away from the window. It imprinted on my heart in ways that followed us both through the next twenty years.

Fast-forward five years to when our children were transitioning back into public schools after being homeschooled for four years. I walked this same boy to his fifth-grade classroom, stopping just short of the door. After only a moment's hesitation, he slipped into the brightly decorated room with the stealth of a ninja. He didn't look back, but I lingered.

I sat in the parking lot for an hour, trying to decide if I should stay—just in case—or go and let him be. Parent drop-off had ended and I was alone in the lot. I could see his classroom window from where I sat. I realized what I was waiting for—his handprints on the glass.

Thirteen years later, we stood—my head only reaching his shoulder—with a jam-packed moving van and the dog nestled safely in the car that would follow. I couldn't believe it was time to go—again. A mist-like rain covered us, and I felt hurried in this good-bye. How many times had I said good-bye? More times than I've recounted here, to be sure. Why is it that each time feels like the last time?

After a tear-filled hug with this now fully grown and fully capable young man, I saw through the car window clearly for the first time. In a last-ditch effort, I wondered once more, should I stay or should I go? But he was fine. And it was time. We pulled out of the parking lot, and I watched him through the car window, with my hand pressed against the glass, as we now moved two thousand miles away, one mile at a time.

One good-bye at a time.

THOUGHT POKE

Letting go is a cumulative process. We have had so much practice up to the point of saying good-bye. Instead of remembering all the times you were parted, can you remember one specific time when you were truly present with your child?

> You, LORD, are a shield around me,
>> my glory, the One who lifts my head
>>> high. (Ps. 3:3)

—

I CAN DO IT ALL BY MYSELF!

But kids don't stay with you if you do it right. It's the one job where, the better you are, the more surely you won't be needed in the long run.

Barbara Kingsolver, *Pigs in Heaven*

The two most common phrases to come out of the mouths of three-year-olds are "Why?" and "I can do it myself." Questioning authority and making your own decisions are hallmarks of adulthood. But it tends to rattle us when the "young adult" is only three feet tall and stands with her hands on her hips and her lower lip pushed out and, once in a while, stomps her feet. Not always getting your way is another grown-up experience; learning to deal with disappointment in an appropriate and healthy way is what makes a grown-up truly worth knowing. Tell that to the mom in the checkout line with a toddler writhing on the grimy linoleum and you just may get slapped!

Our children are well on their way to becoming contributing and productive adults who can care for others even by the age of three. They will test the boundaries, question the status quo, and find ways to step out on their own—as they should. They make plans, carry out those plans, and don't always run their choices by us first. Even Jesus of Nazareth stepped out on his own before his parents were ready (see Luke 2:41–52). I suspect they were surprised more by his independent streak than his detour into the temple. After all, Mary and Joseph probably raised a compliant child who respected his parents and followed the rules.

When our kids step out like that, our first reaction might be to feel disregarded, disrespected, or even rejected. Although rules are meant to be followed and expectations are meant to be met, it's important to double-check whether those rules help our kids grow or squash their development. Without opportunities to pull themselves up, they won't know how to stand and how to walk— without holding our hands. Remember making sure there was a table within reach of your toddlers when they began cruising? At some point they let go and walked into that big empty space of your living room, on their own, with that goofy grin on their faces.

And we all prefer that when our kids let go, they do it with a silly smile and not a look of terror.

THOUGHT POKE

Where are you on the countdown to the big launch? Look for ways to green-light progress and not stop the clock.

> When his parents saw him, they were astonished. His mother said to him, "Son, why have you treated us like this? Your father and I have been anxiously searching for you." (Luke 2:48)

BIG BROTHER (MOTHER) IS WATCHING

*Parents can only give good advice or put them
on the right paths, but the final forming of a
person's character lies in their own hands.*

Anne Frank, *The Diary of a Young Girl*

A headline on social media read, "App shows parents
if their children are attending their college classes—is

this a good way to keep tabs on your kids or is this over the top?" This question is symptomatic of our desire to control every aspect of our children's lives. I admit that if I am paying for my child's college education, I may be tempted to monitor my investment. I might be tempted to ensure that I have access to their college transcripts, their schedule, and the name of the karaoke bar where the organic-chemistry professor, who is the bane of my son's existence, hangs out on Thursday nights. I might be tempted, but I didn't act on it. I didn't even attend the parent sessions during new-student orientation. It was time to let go, and at that time, I wanted my son to have the space I knew he needed.

Did he attend every class? No, he didn't. He some-times told me about it when he didn't. He had all sorts of reasons ranging from "attendance doesn't matter to this professor" to "I have mono"—which he did, by the way, and missed weeks of classes. It was his decision each morning whether or not to go to class. He was the one who had to live with whatever consequences came. Never underestimate the power of natural con-sequences. If you touch the stove, you will get burned.

Natural consequences have the power to curb poor choices or inappropriate behavior better than any artificial consequence that might come from knowing where my son is at all times during his school day.

I will offer a caveat to the college attendance tug-of-war. There are some children who go to college early—that is, they are significantly younger than the typical eighteen or nineteen years old. There are some children who haven't had many, if any, opportunities prior to going to college to manage their own time and make their own choices. And there are some children who are just not developmentally ready to be on their own, yet we dropped them off at their Target-outfitted dorm anyway. We might have to keep a closer eye on them. We might have to let go little by little, and not all at once.

You know your children better than anyone else. You know what they can and can't handle. When deciding how and when to let go or to at least loosen your grip, make sure your decision is based on what they can and can't handle and not on what *you* can and can't handle.

I wish there was an app for that.

THOUGHT POKE

Can you allow your children opportunities to manage their own time, regardless of their age? Can they (not you) live with the natural consequences if they don't handle them well? This goes a long way in teaching them that there is a time for everything.

> There is a time for everything,
>   and a season for every activity under
> the heavens. (Eccles. 3:1)

ALMA MOTHER

We must be willing to get rid of the life we've planned,
so as to have the life that is waiting for us.
Joseph Campbell, *A Joseph Campbell Companion:*
Reflections on the Art of Living

There was a plan. We had a plan. And when I say "we," what I mean to say is "I." I went to college. In fact, I was a first-generation college graduate. My husband, Chip, went to college—he attended four schools on the journey to find himself. I am an educator, and I believed going to college was the best (only?) path. So it was a given that our children would be college bound too. It was a frequent topic of dinnertime conversation throughout their growing up—frequent enough that neither could claim ignorance, but not so frequent that they hid their distaste for it like peas under their mashed potatoes.

Our firstborn went to college; in fact, he attended my alma mater. He lived on campus but was close enough to come home whenever he wanted. I worked on that campus, so he bought me a cup of coffee now and then. His brother was heading the same direction. He was accepted, he had a dorm room reserved, and his first semester's schedule was set. Everything was going according to plan. All that remained was to successfully complete his last semester of his senior year in high school, and then he would start college midsummer, not even waiting for the fall. Getting there wasn't easy. School for Charles was like riding a bicycle through the mud—slow going and taking a lot of energy just to stay upright.

He knew how to ride a bike. But we should have chosen a path made for his type of tires.

The semester came to an end, resulting in a lower-than-expected GPA. His acceptance to college now rescinded, our son was relieved. I, on the other hand, was mystified. He didn't want to go to college?

He wanted to go to technical school. It took a degree of self-sabotage on Charles's part for me to finally see that I needed to let go of my plan so he could embrace his. He needed to choose his own path.

Sometimes what you think is the best choice may not be the right choice. We need to allow our kids to tell us they don't like peas so they don't have to resort to hiding them under their mashed potatoes. What's the worst that could happen? If you offer a variety, they might discover they like another green vegetable instead. In the end, it's their life.

THOUGHT POKE

Is your children's path built for the kind of tires they have? Did they choose the destination? You can trust that God will make their path known to them.

You make known to me the path of life;

you will fill me with joy in your

presence,

with eternal pleasures at your right

hand. (Ps. 16:11)

LORD, SHUT MY MOUTH!

Never miss a good chance to shut up.

Will Rogers

My mother often quoted the saying, "Lord, keep your arm around my shoulders and your hand over my mouth!" She freely admitted that one thing she struggled with as a mom of preteens and young adults was keeping her mouth shut about our choices. She resorted to the silent shaking of the head instead, which in my mind was just as loud. Not as obnoxious as the eye roll, but pretty close.

The struggle is real! How can I not forewarn my sons of the dangers of making poor decisions after a lifetime of living with the consequences of my own lackluster choices? I want to protect them—of course I do. What mother silently stands by and watches as her baby (okay, maybe he's eighteen at this point) walks into a piranha-filled lake with a cut on his hand, completely oblivious to the danger that awaits him? I have to speak up—don't I?

When our younger son played in the band at church, he had found a way to serve that utilized his gifts and talents during the youth service. The leader began to rely on our son more and more, and he occasionally led worship. At eighteen years old, this was a great boost to his confidence and helped him make a connection to his faith that he had been struggling with. I marveled at his grace during worship and truly reveled in his talent. It made the service that much sweeter when our son led worship. My pride was full to bursting. As I look back, that should have been a red flag to me.

Then along came a girl. My husband reminds me that it's always about a girl. Did you know, ladies, that we have the power to disrupt, distract, and even derail guys from the path they were set to follow—for better or for worse? We talk often about how we need to protect our girls from guys who will lead them astray. When we talk to our girls about how they might lead guys astray, we need to explain the *why* along with the *how*.

"It's all about those womanly wiles," Chip explains. "Or maybe we're just like dogs. We may be faithfully walking on a leash with our masters and then—squirrel!"

I saw her, and it was as if there was a neon sign flashing over her head that read "Trouble." I wanted to run to my son, hands waving wildly just like the robot in *Lost in Space*—yelling, "Danger, Will Robinson, danger!" But I sat on those very hands. I watched and waited and hoped he would see her for what she was and not be distracted. Keep your hand over my mouth, Lord!

When this young lady finally walked out of my son's life, he then walked away from the worship band and the church. He was broken. I feared his faith was broken as well. Although I had uttered some sound yet unsolicited words of wisdom (at least I thought they were wise) during this distracting time in my son's life, he did not have ears to hear them. I don't know what really happened. The mother-son relationship is intact. I worry, though, that the Father-child one is not as strong as it once was. Should I have said more? Should I have taken a stand against the young lady in his life? That word *should*—we need to do something about that too.

My own mother was silent when I allowed a boy to change my thinking about church. She waited in prayer for years for my return. Whether it's about a boy or about a girl, sometimes we allow this distraction to derail us intstead.

It's not really a matter of keeping our mouths shut. It's more a matter of choosing our words wisely and asking the Spirit to guide our tongues when we do speak—if we must speak. It's important not to have regret for words left unsaid. We just need to be thoughtful about which words we parse out to those we love.

I choose to believe that my husband is right about guys and girls. We may get distracted by a squirrel, but we are still on the leash, still tethered to God, whether or not we realize it.

THOUGHT POKE

Each choice our children make is an opportunity to speak wisdom into their lives. Just be mindful that you don't speak unadvisedly. Do you give yourself time to think before you speak? Be slow to speak, if you speak at all.

> My dear brothers and sisters, take note of this: Everyone should be quick to listen, slow to speak and slow to become angry. (James 1:19)

Day 7

MOTHER'S CURSE

Children have never been very good at listening to their
elders, but they have never failed to imitate them.

James Baldwin, *Nobody Knows My Name*

"I hope you have a child just like you!"

Every mother since the beginning of time has pro-
nounced this to her teenage or young-adult children
as she struggled to make sense of this alien being who
somehow shared her home, last name, and, oh yeah,
looked just like her. I remember thinking it wouldn't be

so bad if I had a child like me. I laughed, believing my mother was confused (my first mistake); surely what she meant as a curse would actually be a blessing.

And then I had children.

And then they grew up.

Along the way they did things contrary to how I thought I'd raised them.

Raising children is a mix of the spoken and the unspoken. Children learn more from what you do than from what you say. All the parenting experts say so. I said so when asked on radio and television interviews. And I believed it.

It appears we all need to be a little more explicit.

Our goal was to raise critical and creative thinkers who wouldn't be led down the wrong path or follow empty promises. We taught our children to question everything, to be confident in their choices, and to do no harm. We reinforced that you had to be able to take care of yourself before you could take care of another person (spouse or child). We wanted them to be interdependent—able to depend on others yet stand on their own.

When our older son decided to get married, I shuddered. They weren't getting married in a church. Gulp. They weren't being married by a priest or pastor. Um, why not? The wedding invitations didn't mention either set of parents. Hold the phone! What's going on here? What happened to everything we taught you about what should happen when you get married?

I realized, much to my dismay, that we had never outlined any of those expectations out loud. They were part of the unspoken.

Our son had grown into exactly what we wanted him to be—a critical thinker, independent, questioning the status quo, and doing no harm. Except, obviously, I felt hurt, so harm had been done. Right?

Nostalgic, I pulled out our wedding album, set on reminiscing about the kind of wedding my son would never have. And then I saw it. Our wedding invitation: "Chip and Vicki invite you ..." And that's when I heard my mother giggle from heaven—satisfied that her curse had come true.

I had a child just like me. But I've decided I was right all along—he's a blessing.

THOUGHT POKE

Can you recognize yourself in your child's choices? Think of a time when that recognition gave you hope. There's hope that our children will return to what they know.

> "There is hope for your descendants,"
> declares the LORD.
> "Your children will return to their
> own land." (Jer. 31:17)

Day 8

———

WHAT'S FOR DINNER?

Success is not counted by how high you have climbed
but by how many people you brought with you.

Wil Rose

My friend Betsy swooped into my office for a closed-door conversation, clutching her phone and then exhaling with a huff.

"I'm so confused," she began. "I thought my girls might be anxious about being left alone until I get home tonight, but the only thing they're worried about is what I will bring home for dinner."

Betsy and her husband are testing the waters by leaving their twelve-year-old twins alone after school for a few hours until one or the other gets home from work. Deciding that after-school care is no longer necessary or financially feasible, this mother of two preteen girls had mixed feelings about this rite of passage.

"I know this is one of those steps toward independence, but secretly, I think I hoped they would not want to be alone, that they would still need me to be there as they came home to an empty house and did their homework and the list of chores I'd left for them," Betsy confessed.

"Well, they seem to need you to bring them dinner," I said. "That's something."

On the one hand, we are actively preparing our children for adulthood; on the other, we're holding on to still being needed. It's a tricky balance. We want them to make their own money to buy their own clothes (or video games) yet feel left out when we no longer get to go shopping with them. We hurry them to get their driver's licenses but then realize we aren't always in the loop about where they've taken the car. We push them to complete their college applications and then stare longingly into their childhood rooms come fall.

Every step forward our children take is one more step away from us. It's tempting to watch them go down that road and panic by pulling them back. Betsy was tempted.

"I think maybe it's too soon to leave them alone," she told me. "I mean, they're only twelve, and they still have so much to learn, right?"

I just smiled and didn't say what I was really thinking. What I was really thinking was maybe it's time they learn to cook for themselves—and while they're at it, have dinner ready for *you* when you get home. But Betsy wasn't ready to hear that.

And I'm glad I didn't open my mouth.

"No," she said and answered her own question. "It's time. They're ready. It's me who's not quite ready. I need to get over that."

And she will. We all will.

After we figure out what to bring home for dinner.

THOUGHT POKE

Does the journey toward independence feel like tug-of-war? Instead of seeing it that way, how about looking at it more like rock climbing—your child is the lead climber and you are down below, belaying rope as needed and determining points of protection.

> Be ready to do whatever is good.
> (Titus 3:1)

——

FINANCIAL AID

Give me six hours to chop down a tree and I
will spend the first four sharpening the axe.

Often attributed to Abraham Lincoln

Social media has quickly become the great reminder
of all kinds of important dates and tasks. Just today I
received four birthday reminders, a doctor's appointment reminder, a reminder to post to my blog (which
has been lonely for a couple of months now), and since
it's January, I've been reminded that it is FAFSA time.

Parents spend years preparing their children for what is called "post-secondary" life. As a teacher I used the term *college-and-career readiness*. In other words, are our children prepared for an independent life after they graduate from high school? That means they call the shots. That means I will no longer be their chauffeur (as long as they can afford their own car and insurance). That means whatever they choose to do with their lives, they have the means to achieve it.

Yet I'm the one taking out the PLUS loans to support their post-secondary plans.

Even though Chip and I strive to ensure our boys can stand on their own two feet, there are still times when they are standing on ours—like when my father taught me how to dance and I stood on his feet so I could learn the steps. We go through the motions together until they are able to remember which step to take first and the order of the next steps. For some of us the dance is more complicated than the box step and takes longer to learn. For others it's more about the fact that one or the other of us is not as naturally coordinated and makes missteps. That's me.

When it comes to preparing our sons for financial freedom (freedom from the need of Mom and Dad's money), I've learned that it's not as straightforward sure-footed as a financial planner might lead you to believe. It's nuanced and responsive—more like ballet and less like line dancing. They need to learn the steps of saving for the future, curbing impulse buying, and monitoring their spending on a daily basis. There are many digital tools to order these steps. We can help our children by engaging in money management with them well before they earn that first paycheck.

THOUGHT POKE

Remember that sometimes God's providence for your children's struggle to stand on their own is you. Sometimes the letting go is how God will provide; sometimes it's the holding on. Can you bring to mind a time when your letting go was exactly what your children needed?

> My God will meet all your needs according to the riches of his glory in Christ Jesus. (Phil. 4:19)

CAREFUL PREPARATION

Be honest when you are with your kids, because you see your past in their eyes and they see their future in yours.

Nishan Panwar

Teaching on a college campus makes me a witness to how well college-bound teens have been prepared to live and learn away from home. According to *U.S. News & World Report*, as many as one out of three freshmen doesn't make it to his or her sophomore year.[1] The reasons run the gamut from family problems and loneliness to academic struggles and lack of money. If schools you're considering have low freshman-retention rates, you'll want to ask the admissions office why. Some colleges do a great job of taking care of their freshmen; some don't. Then again, I wonder if it is solely up to colleges to ensure retention of their students.

Nikki showed up to our campus knitting club teary-eyed and weary. "I think I'm going to transfer," she said to her fellow lovers of all things yarn. "I may even leave before the semester is over."

I'd heard this from Nikki before. In fact, she had made this same statement every week for the past six weeks. I knew there was more to it than freshman-year fears. Yes, it was her first time away from home. Yes, she wasn't the strongest student. That was true for many of our students. She wasn't unique, but it became clear that she was quite special to her mom.

---

1   "Freshman Retention Rate," *U.S. News & World Report*, http://
colleges.usnews.rankingsandreviews.com/best-colleges/rankings/
national-universities/freshmen-least-most-likely-return.

The only child of a single mother, Nikki was and continues to be her mom's best friend. They depend on each other for companionship and emotional support. Although Nikki's mom was proud of her daughter's acceptance to college and did everything she could to help her move into her dorm by outfitting it to the envy of those around her, Nikki's mom began to regret letting her daughter go so far away from home (in reality, she was forty-five minutes away). Nightly phone calls and daily texts revealing her distress at being alone began to cause high levels of anxiety in Nikki. Her classwork suffered from the emotional distraction, and then her own loneliness settled in like fog on San Francisco Bay.

It didn't matter that her roommates encouraged her to stay, nor did it make a difference that her professors, advisers, and coaches supported her as a learner. Nikki was unable to function away from her mom because her mom was unable to function away from Nikki. A word of encouragement from her mother would have dissipated that fog of anxiety.

Nikki left two weeks before the end of the semester.

Our children aren't the only ones who need to prepare for their leaving home. We must prepare ourselves as well.

As their need for independence increases, our need for dependence should decrease.

THOUGHT POKE

Missing our children when they leave us is natural. Depending on their presence for our own well-being can suffocate their confidence. What words of encouragement can you give your children today so you are better able to let them go tomorrow?

> Anxiety weighs down the heart, but a
> kind word cheers it up. (Prov. 12:25)

Day 11

FREE RANGERS

You become responsible forever for what you've tamed.
Antoine de Saint-Exupéry, *The Little Prince*

A 2012 study of 438 college students in the *Journal of Adolescence* reported that because of limited opportunities for emerging adults to practice and develop important skills needed for becoming self-reliant adults, college students reported higher levels of depression and less satisfaction in life.[1] Two of our basic psychological needs are *autonomy* and *competence*. I know we wanted both for our boys, but I started to wonder whether we had given them what they needed to reach both.

Preparing our kids for college and career is a near-sighted goal. What about life beyond the classroom or the boardroom? As a special-education teacher, I spent a great deal of time teaching my students life skills and all the independent decision making that goes along with them. I had to teach them those skills because they were not naturally developing or their home environment did not actively support those skills. But these were students with disabilities, so it follows that typical kids shouldn't need that sort of teaching. Right?

Unfortunately, we have raised a generation of kids in highly structured childhoods with few decision-making opportunities. We've orchestrated every moment. They are like caged chickens—only eating what is provided and

---

1   Laura M. Padilla-Walker and Larry J. Nelson, "Black Hawk Down? Establishing Helicopter Parenting as a Distinct Construct from Other Forms of Parental Control during Emerging Adulthood," *Journal of Adolescence* 35, no. 5 (2012): 1177–90.

limited to a small footprint of space. My fear was that my kids would think they couldn't make decisions without me. I want them to be able to take care of themselves and someday their own families. I can't do that for them, nor should I.

When our sons were flying home for the holidays, they discovered their flight had been delayed to such an extent that they would miss their connection and then be stranded in Atlanta for two days. Both separately got on the phone with the airline and problem-solved another way home. Fiercely yet respectfully, they each insisted the airline find them a way home.

That night, before giving in to long-awaited sleep (it had been a long day), I said to Chip, "They figured it out."

"And they didn't ask me for help," Chip replied.

That is what made us proud.

Questioning is one of the most effective ways to teach children problem-solving skills. Instead of telling them how to do it, ask them in what ways they might solve the problem. The solutions they generate may be different than yours would be, but that's what will make them invest in them. Their problems, their solutions.

THOUGHT POKE

We have been given a spirit of power and self-control, not of fear. Can we give our children that same spirit by letting them roam on their own? The next time your children face a problem, encourage them to come up with their own solutions.

> The Spirit God gave us does not make us timid, but gives us power, love and self-discipline. (2 Tim. 1:7)

Day 12

———

SEND THEM PACKING

Travel makes a wise Man better, but a Fool worse.

Thomas Fuller, *Gnomologia*

We traveled enough while the boys were growing up that packing for even an overnight at Nana and Pop Pop's house became pretty efficient work. As the one who did the packing, I knew what we needed and didn't need on any particular trip. I may not be good at wrapping presents (as my family lovingly knows), but I'm a great packer!

It's interesting to watch as your kids shift from being dependent on Mom and Dad to becoming dependent on themselves. On a recent trip I held back as our son tried to determine whether his bag was under the airline's fifty-pound limit to avoid the overweight penalty. He knew any overages were coming out of his own pocket, not mine.

After unsuccessfully trying to weigh the luggage on our bathroom scale, he picked it up and stepped on the scale himself. I had no idea how much my full-grown son actually weighed, so this was interesting. Doing the math, he decided his bag came just under the fifty-pound weight limit.

"Just in case," he explained, "I'm not going to take back the vintage Nintendo 64 system we found at the antique store. Can you keep it here for me?"

Within seconds a not-so-enticing possible future flashed before me—the beginning of a habit of storing their stuff at my house for an indeterminate amount of time, which I would regret as our garage space filled with things they weren't quite ready to store for themselves. Having been the default storage unit for my siblings as they moved out on their own, I wasn't interested in becoming that again, even for our own children. We were in the process of downsizing, so storing more stuff wasn't part of the plan.

I proposed an alternative: "Find out the difference in cost between paying the weight overage and shipping the Nintendo 64 to yourself. Then decide how to handle it. You can ship it out today on the way to the airport if necessary," I suggested, with the expectation that this was his problem to solve, not mine.

Needless to say, we did not stop at the post office on our way to the airport, and much to my son's satisfaction, his bag weighed forty-eight pounds, as expected.

THOUGHT POKE

How well prepared are your kids for the journey ahead? Do they know what to take and what to leave behind? Part of our adult journey is forgetting what lies behind and reaching for what is ahead. In what ways can you help your child do the same?

I press on to take hold of that for which
Christ Jesus took hold of me. Brothers
and sisters, I do not consider myself yet
to have taken hold of it. But one thing
I do: Forgetting what is behind and
straining toward what is ahead, I press
on toward the goal to win the prize for
which God has called me heavenward in
Christ Jesus. (Phil. 3:12–14)

THE CHICK
THAT FELL OUT
OF THE NEST

Character cannot be developed in ease and quiet. Only through experience of trial and suffering can the soul be strengthened, ambition inspired, and success achieved.

Helen Keller

"I don't want to do this," she said between sobs. "I just don't want to be here."

I held her registration form in my hands. We'd picked out her classes for next semester, and even though Kallie wanted to go back to her high school and drop out of our early-college program, it was my job to register her for the next semester.

"I've talked to them both over and over again," she said. "They don't understand. I'm just not ready to be here. It's too much. It's all too much!"

"This looks like a much better schedule this time," I said, pointing to the printout. "I think you'll enjoy it if you give it a chance."

She ignored my encouragement.

"What can I do to get thrown out of this program?" she asked with a sly smile, knowing she'd get a rise out of me. Yet she was that desperate.

"Don't jeopardize your future by doing something stupid," I said. I was wearing my "mom hat" now. The thing was—I agreed. I knew Kallie was not ready for this transition to early college. After all, it's not for everyone.

As parents, we believe we know what's best for our children and hate it when someone tells us differently— even when it's our own children telling us. It's hard to let them make their own decisions about what's best for them when we're used to making those decisions for them.

How do you know when it's time? How do you know when to shove the baby birds out of the nest and when to hold them back away from the edge? It may be too comfortable for them in that nest. Without a good shove, they'll never learn how to fly for themselves.

Right now, Kallie's view of her nest is from the ground. She may need to be hand-fed and protected a little more than the rest if she doesn't get back into the nest. Or she may discover that she is indeed strong enough to fly—she just won't know until she tries.

Her parents know her better than I do, and all I can do is show her the way and keep the predators away. The rest is up to her.

THOUGHT POKE

How comfortable is your nest? Some of our chicks out-grow it faster than others. Remember to consider your child's maturity and competence and not just your own comfort in that nest. Pray that God will fill them with the knowledge of his will.

> Since the day we heard about you, we have not stopped praying for you. We continually ask God to fill you with the knowledge of his will through all the wisdom and understanding that the Spirit gives, so that you may live a life worthy of the Lord and please him in every way: bearing fruit in every good work, growing in the knowledge of God. (Col. 1:9–10)

FIRST-JOB FRUSTRATIONS

When we are no longer able to change a situation …
we are challenged to change ourselves.

Viktor Frankl, *Man's Search for Meaning*

"I want a different job," our younger son, Charles, said at age sixteen when he came home from work. He was a server in the dining room of a retirement village near our home. His brother worked there as well but in a different building.

"What happened this time?" I asked.

"My manager just yells at me for no reason. I feel targeted. It's like I can't do anything right." He was frustrated, and I would've been too.

He was already on the hunt for a new job when he voiced his ever-increasing anxiety. He'd been there for only three months. His particular position had a high turnover rate. Kids were coming and going all the time. I'm sure it was just as frustrating for the manager as it was for the employees. But we had a golden opportunity to help our son navigate this turmoil and not run from it.

We all prefer the path of least resistance, but it doesn't often lead us where we want to go. Perseverance and a strong work ethic can overcome a multitude of job-related frustrations. But how do you encourage your teens to stick it out when all they want to do is quit?

We realized our son wasn't prepared to handle some challenges in that job, and we addressed those first. He didn't know the words to use when he was asked to do something unethical or not part of his job (like work overtime for nothing or hide a mistake that could hurt someone). He didn't know how to look busy when he had nothing to do (checking his phone was not acceptable).

And he didn't know how to work with difficult personalities without letting it affect his job performance. We could guide him through those issues, but we couldn't, nor should we, do it for him. If the situation got out of hand or if there were safety, health, or legal consequences because of bad management, then of course we would have stepped in.

As tempted as we are to run interference for our kids in their first and subsequent jobs, it's crucial that they learn how to stand up for themselves. This is the perfect time to give them the tools they need and then send them out to practice on their own.

THOUGHT POKE

Do you have a first-job memory you can share that illustrates some of these concerns? Think of a time when you've had to submit to a boss even though you didn't want to. However you handled it way back when doesn't matter. What matters now is how you'll help your teen handle it.

> Give back to Caesar what is Caesar's, and
> to God what is God's. (Matt. 22:21)

MILESTONES OR MILLSTONES?

My path has not been determined. I shall have more experiences and pass many more milestones.

Agnetha Fältskog

I was so relieved! Our older son, Christopher, finished a five-and-a-half-hour drive to his aunt and uncle's house in Tallahassee—by himself! He's a good driver, and he'd driven it before, following one of us in his own car, but that day he left the house for the weekend on his own to serve as sponsor for his cousin at his confirmation. As most of us with teenage drivers know, this is a frightening prospect, but it is a milestone and one I'm glad we've reached. After all, driving almost three hundred miles by yourself is something to be proud of.

He stopped and called me every hour and a half to check in, and it helped ease my anxious heart. Without cruise control in his car, keeping his foot on the accelerator that long made for sore muscles the next day. I guess he didn't realize he was anxious about this trip as well. He was about to turn eighteen, and the milestones were coming fast and furious, just as they did when he was an infant, baby, and toddler. We'd taught him so much ... but had we taught him enough?

Milestones are a series of numbered markers placed along a road boundary at intervals of one mile. Many of the milestones we experience with our children are captured or recorded and often celebrated in some way; they are the mile markers. This particular milestone in our son's life was not recorded and shared on social media. None of my friends were bombarded with a minute-by-minute account of my son's road trip. He didn't check in virtually so I could monitor his progress on my computer. This milestone, like so many, had me on my knees, praying for a successful outcome—by myself.

Sometimes our presence at every milestone, with our hands in the air cheering our children on, might make the milestone dependent on our presence. Our kids may have to meet their milestones on their own and without fanfare. Our quiet affirmation of them should be enough for them to move forward on their journey.

There's a chance that when we insist on being right there for every moment, we just get in the way of their progress.

THOUGHT POKE

Being there for every moment may cause your children to stumble on their journey. Respect the milestone so you don't become a millstone instead.

> If anyone causes one of these little ones—
> those who believe in me—to stumble, it

would be better for them to have a large millstone hung around their neck and to be drowned in the depths of the sea. (Matt. 18:6)

Day 16

FREEDOM ISN'T FREE

*Nothing is more difficult, and therefore more
precious, than to be able to decide.*

Napoleon Bonaparte

I asked one of my former students what it was like during
her freshman year of college. Alyssa explained it to me
this way:

> The word *freedom* cannot be completely
> understood until the first night in college.

There are no parents to check in with, no curfews, and not nearly as many rules as back at home. I grew up in a very strict household throughout high school. I had to always tell my parents exactly what I would be doing at every minute of my night, which was interrupted by at least four or five phone calls. Since I've gotten here, I have experienced more freedom than I ever thought possible. I went downtown with a group of people until 1:00 a.m. and didn't have to justify to my mother that we were being safe. I walk to go buy a cup of Starbucks coffee without my dad telling me I could feed someone a meal with the money I was going to spend. I've done my laundry after midnight some days because I was playing Rock Band in a guy's room with a group of people, which my parents would consider unacceptable.

However, with freedom comes responsibility. There have been nights where I have stayed up until 3:00 a.m. talking with people—the night before I have class. However, I have done my homework for the night and still wake up and am attentive in class. Freedom is only a gift if a student accepts the responsibility that goes along with college life. Procrastination is inevitable for most, and I am definitely not the exception. Sometimes ordering Chinese food and watching *House* seems way more fulfilling than writing an eight-page paper for my theology class. However, the biggest lesson I've learned is that I can appreciate the freedom more once I have completed all my responsibilities.

Each decision made on her own led to making the next decision on her own. Alyssa began to trust her instincts with the full realization that not every choice would be the right choice—but it was her choice, and that's what mattered. The next decision took her even farther away. After college she moved to South Korea to teach English. Watching her flourish in this farther-away-than-I-could-imagine landscape made my ovaries hurt! A thousand degrees of separation! She might as well be living on the moon.

Sometimes confidence and competence come with distance.

THOUGHT POKE

How close do you have to be to your children to let them go? Sometimes they become far-flung as a reaction to our often-too-close proximity. We can back away gracefully so they don't feel they have to push us away.

> From everyone who has been given much,
> much will be demanded; and from the
> one who has been entrusted with much,
> much more will be asked. (Luke 12:48)

Day 17

TWO STEPS FORWARD, ONE STEP BACK

"Why were you searching for me?" he asked. "Didn't you know I had to be in my Father's house?" But they did not understand what he was saying to them.

Luke 2:49–50

Living *with* your parents and living *for* your parents are two different realities. I compare it to living to eat versus eating to live. The healthy habit is eating to live, if you were wondering. Although if chocolate mousse is involved, that thinking may go right out the window for me.

That first summer home from college can be a tipping point in many families. The balance of power and control is tested, and what many don't realize in the moment is that as a result this may be the last summer your child lives at home with you. If the college your child attends doesn't offer summer classes, I strongly encourage them to look for summer internships, study-abroad programs, or mission trips to fill that gap. Independence doesn't happen in your childhood bedroom with your mom cooking all your meals and your dad putting gas in your car every week. It comes from going away and being separate.

When Payge returned from her summer study-abroad experience, she had some difficulty with re-entry for the last couple of weeks at home before the fall term started. She was so used to being on her own while in New Zealand that she resented every way her mom tried to take care of her. She even resented that her mom did her laundry. What college kid hates that her mom does her laundry? Feeling like the three-year-old who stands with her hands on her hips and announces, "I can do it myself!" Payge found a way to start her job on campus a week early and left for school. Her mom felt rejected and complained to her girlfriends that her daughter had gotten "too big for her britches."

When our kids are ready to fly, it's counterproductive to make them stay in the nest. It's cruel to clip their wings! Some may not come back. That's a hard truth to accept as a parent. The longing for a life of their own outweighs their need to please us. And in reality, that's how it should be.

THOUGHT POKE

Are there places in your kids' lives where you are holding on too tightly? Can you release your grip so those places become more about them and less about you?

> Then he went down to Nazareth with them and was obedient to them. But his mother treasured all these things in her heart. (Luke 2:51)

Day 18

———

WORK IN PROGRESS

All men make mistakes, but only wise
men learn from their mistakes.
Winston Churchill

As a teacher and a parent, I've always struggled with trying
to help students gain organizational and time-management
skills. Maybe you've found yourself faced with this at 9:00
p.m. on a Sunday night: "Mom, I need three different colors
of poster board, one hundred multicolored pushpins, and

duct tape [who is he, MacGyver?]—like now. My project's due tomorrow!"

He waited until the last minute—again. Now you're wondering if there is a twenty-four-hour Walgreens somewhere within the greater metropolitan area, and you're just too tired to move. Part of you whispers in your ear, "Let him fail. Then maybe he'll learn his lesson!" and the other part of you says, "Good moms don't let their kids fail."

It's a matter of accountability. Whose responsibility is it to complete the project? Who is getting the grade?

I know it sounds simpler than it really is—believe me. I've had my share of late nights and panicked morning rides to school with my sons. I get tired of always being the one who is aware of what my kids need to get done—when they don't *seem* to have a clue. I already completed seventh grade—why should I do it again?

Take a look at this online exchange from some real students in seventh grade—gifted students, by the way. Their names have been changed, but the spirit of the conversation is accurate. They know when things are due. Don't let them fool you.

They are messaging about a huge assignment that is due the next morning:

> **Ellie:** I just finished Mr. Meeko's stupid essay, like 640 words :/ hating this project right now

> **Cathy:** Haha I didn't even start it :/

> **Ellie:** wooooow, theres a shock (;

> **Lisa:** todd hasnt even started too

> **Ellie:** wooow (;

> **Lisa:** i fished mine like an hour ago r we suppose to have a biblio

> **Ellie:** yeah , that's the websites right ?

> **Lisa:** i didnt do that

Cathy: Yeah it is

Ellie: in alphebetical order.

Lisa: im doing it on the final copy

Our children, just like our projects, are all a work in progress. They need to be held accountable.

THOUGHT POKE

One of the best things you can do is help your children keep track of their own progress. Find ways to do that with your kids. It makes the difference. But don't keep track for them. You are competent to instruct in this way.

> I myself am convinced, my brothers and sisters, that you yourselves are full of goodness, filled with knowledge and competent to instruct one another. (Rom. 15:14)

LETTING GO, GIVING IN, AND ALL THE REST

Letting go doesn't mean that you don't care about someone anymore. It's just realizing that the only person you really have control over is yourself.

Deborah Reber, *Chicken Soup for the Teenage Soul: The Real Deal Challenges*

I taught sixth graders—middle schoolers in the midst of one of their biggest transitions in life so far. They are, by definition, in the middle of their transition to adulthood.

Their hormones are all over the place, and they are no longer babies, but they are not quite grown enough to be on their own. Parents don't know how to hold on, how to let go, or how not to hover.

The preadolescent is a unique being but also a recent phenomenon. The term *teenager* didn't even enter our lexicon until 1941. In the first part of the twentieth century, we made a startling discovery: there were teenagers among us! Until then, we had thought of people in just two stages: children and adults. And while childhood might have its tender moments, the goal of the child was to grow up as promptly as possible in order to enjoy the opportunities and shoulder the responsibilities of an adult. The girl became the woman; the boy became the man. It was as simple and significant as that.

Today, parents of preteens, teens, and young adults struggle with what past generations took for granted—the girl becomes the woman; the boy becomes the man.

Going from dependence to independence is as worrisome for our eighteen-year-olds as it is for their parents. The uncertainty connects us, but it also divides us, as we have different views on how to deal with it.

Our source of insight and advice has to go beyond *The Secret Life of the American Teenager*—it's time for us to think about how we let go, sometimes give in, and all the rest.

THOUGHT POKE

What are you most concerned about as a parent trying to prepare your kids to fly on their own? What frustrates you most in your attempt to give them wings?

> Let us discern for ourselves what is
>   right;
> let us learn together what is good.
>   (Job 34:4)

LEARNING HOW TO SHIFT

*Life is like riding a bicycle. To keep your
balance you must keep moving.*

Albert Einstein

Learning how to drive a stick shift in my thirties was uncomfortable, to say the least. That moment of physical transition when you release the clutch and shift, hoping you won't stall, is full of uncertainty for me—sort of like being in limbo.

No, I'm not talking about the supposed waiting room of heaven. I'm talking about the times when you feel a little uncertain, a little in limbo. These are the moments of lull when you might change your mind about what you thought you were going to do. You might feel something is worse than it actually is—like mistaking a bunny for a python.

Right now, I am in limbo. I choose to put myself in this place more often than I probably should. After all, I'm the one making the changes, making a new decision, or entering unfamiliar territory. I realized, however, that everyone is in a state of limbo—we are all *becoming*. Sometimes we have control over this; other times it is involuntary—something we just have to go through. The more I think about how uncomfortable things are, the more uncomfortable they become—like learning to drive a stick shift.

Our children want to stand on their own but still be taken care of. We want them to fly but still be safe in our nest. When you are in transition, the worst thing that can happen is to find yourself alone.

Even if you are the one struggling through limbo right now, there's probably someone else in your life you may not have noticed who is even more uncomfortable. Maybe there is a mom whose son is in rebellion and disappears for days at a time, or maybe your best girlfriend has cried every day since her daughter went to college only two towns over. Can you be there next to them and put your hand on theirs and show them when to shift into first?

THOUGHT POKE

Be mindful of those around you. Shifting is much easier when you have a hand to hold on to. Even the apostles were there to help one another wait in that upper room for the ultimate shift.

> The apostles returned to Jerusalem from the hill called the Mount of Olives, a Sabbath day's walk from the city. When they arrived, they went upstairs to the room where they were staying. Those present were Peter, John, James and Andrew; Philip and Thomas, Bartholomew and Matthew; James son of Alphaeus and

Simon the Zealot, and Judas son of James. They all joined together constantly in prayer, along with the women and Mary the mother of Jesus, and with his brothers. (Acts 1:12–14)

———

RIDING THE BUS
WITH MY SIBLINGS

*"For I know the plans I have for you," declares
the L*ORD*, "plans to prosper you and not to harm
you, plans to give you hope and a future."*
Jeremiah 29:11

My parents' fifteenth wedding anniversary was coming up, and as the oldest of five, I took it upon myself to surprise them with a gift from their children. Since crystal is the traditional gift for fifteen years of wedded bliss (although they might have disputed the blissful part), I created an elaborate plan for us to save up for and purchase a crystal serving bowl that would go nicely with the other beautiful things in my mother's china cabinet. We ranged in age from fourteen down to six; each of us agreed to save our birthday money from the year toward this very grown-up gift.

But raising the money was only half the battle. It was to be a surprise. I needed to find a way to get to the store on my own without our parents knowing. I grew up in an urban environment where public transportation was king. I knew how to get around on my own but now needed to find a way to do that with my four siblings in tow and without assistance. With forty dollars saved toward the crystal bowl, I told my mom I would take everyone to our neighborhood pool for the afternoon. I'd done it before, so she was none the wiser. We rode our bikes to the bus stop, chained them up, and then caught the 1:15 bus to the center of town near Jonelle's Jewelers. Herding my siblings first to the bus, then onto the bus and to the jeweler was no easy feat for this fourteen-year-old. Once at the store, each of us emptied our pockets of our birthday cash and pointed to the crisscross-cut crystal bowl on display. We made it home on the 2:00 bus with time to spare to still go to the pool.

Our parents were both thrilled and proud of our ability to pull off this surprise. They weren't mad that we sneaked out to the bus, nor were they frightened for us traveling alone. Their pride in us empowered each of us to move forward on our own—even my then six-year-old brother whose wobbly bike ride to the bus stop made me continually look back to be sure he was still with us.

Our children's ability to make a plan and execute that plan on their own is something we need to make room for as parents. Great ideas are only that—ideas—until they are put into action. That crystal bowl now resides in my own china cabinet since my beautiful mom left this earth. Every time I see that bowl, I'm reminded of how she made room in her life for my plans.

THOUGHT POKE

Sometimes it's hard to leave the plan up to others. They might disappoint us. In fact, there's a good chance they will. But without the opportunity to make and execute their own plans, their future is stuck in our past. Can you make room in your life for your children's plans?

> You will call on me and come and pray
> to me, and I will listen to you. You will
> seek me and find me when you seek me
> with all your heart. (Jer. 29:12–13)

Day 22

LIFEBLOOD

As we let our own light shine, we unconsciously
give other people permission to do the same.
As we are liberated from our own fear, our
presence automatically liberates others.
Marianne Williamson, *A Return to Love*

The late-teen years are full of milestones and rites of passage. Sometimes we don't even recognize them as such. I've been blessed with the opportunity to both live with and work with high-school-age kids. Sometimes they seem so clueless; other times they spout the wisdom of those way beyond their years.

On one particular night, my sixteen-year-old son, Charles, said, "Mom, could you sign this form allowing me to give blood tomorrow at school?"

"Why? Why now?" I asked.

"I've always wanted to do this. I just think it's time," he responded maturely.

His father, who has a rare blood type, gives blood as often as he is allowed. He believes he has a responsibility to do so since he was created with such a rare type. Our sons have seen this ritual played out their entire lives. So I signed on the dotted line. He gave blood during third period.

According to my baby boy (all six feet, one inch and two hundred pounds of him), passing out on the way out of the bloodmobile wasn't as bad as he thought. The attendants recognized the look immediately and set him in a wheelchair before he could hit the concrete. They gave him more Powerade and other sugar-filled food, and within a few minutes he looked less ghostlike.

Part of this was my fault. I didn't make sure he ate a good breakfast that morning, and I didn't warn him about the perils of donating blood. But that wasn't the only surprise.

"They asked me really weird questions," he told me later. "I can't even bring myself to tell you."

"You mean they asked you about your sexual activity," I said. I'd given blood before, so I knew.

"Yeah," he said, suddenly relieved. "They asked for all the way back to 1998! What are they thinking?" Charles was seven in 1998.

"It's the law. They have to. Since the outbreak of AIDS, they have to be careful. They test all the blood."

"But what if people lie?" he asked. "People's lives are on the line."

They are indeed. Blood is life. Giving blood gives life. Giving when it's not asked of you is grace. My son was proud of choosing to give that day. In the picture I snapped, he stands tall and strong as the superheroes he idolizes, even if he was still a little woozy.

THOUGHT POKE

If your children ask permission to give, consider saying yes. Giving out of their abundance may be the way they will supply what someone else needs. Let go of your own discomfort or fear so they might embrace courage.

> Our desire is not that others might be relieved while you are hard pressed, but that there might be equality. At the present time your plenty will supply what they need, so that in turn their plenty will supply what you need. The goal is equality, as it is written: "The one who gathered much did not have too much, and the one who gathered little did not have too little." (2 Cor. 8:13–15)

ON MY HONOR, I WILL DO MY BEST

By failing to prepare, you are preparing to fail.

Often attributed to Benjamin Franklin

Our younger son went to the Windy City one week-end in ninth grade—without us! At fifteen years old, he got on an airplane with forty of his closest friends and eight chaperones to compete in a choral competition in Chicago.

The jury was out on how well he would handle himself out there (we'd know in two more days), but he'd made a great start. He packed on his own the night before. He made himself a written checklist of what not to forget in the morning. He got himself up at 4:00 a.m. to be at school by 5:00 a.m. to leave for the airport. He remembered his cell-phone charger. He remembered his asthma inhaler. He remembered to check his luggage tags for the correct address (we'd recently moved).

And off he went.

We've trained them over the years how to travel on their own. After all, that is the goal—that they will be able to take care of themselves. As parents we need to work ourselves out of a job. Here's the progression we use to train our kids to stand on their own:

1. Show them how it's done—model it for them (i.e., I used to pack *for* him).
2. Do it with them—guide them through it (i.e., I packed *with* him).

3. Watch them do it—supervise them as they do it on their own (i.e., I watched *him* pack).

4. Let them do it themselves—independence! (i.e., he packed *on his own*).

Does this mean he didn't forget anything? Probably not. We all forget something when we pack—why wouldn't he? Does this mean he was ready to go out into the big, bad world? Not yet, but he was well on his way. If he were a Boy Scout, he would have earned a badge for packing. But as his Scout leader, I would have been the one to teach him how to pack.

THOUGHT POKE

Whether or not you were a Boy or Girl Scout, you can ask yourself how well prepared your kids are to do things on their own. What types of badges have they earned so far?

The LORD is my shepherd, I lack
nothing.
He makes me lie down in green
pastures,
he leads me beside quiet waters,
he refreshes my soul.
He guides me along the right paths
for his name's sake. (Ps. 23:1–3)

—

DO NOT ENTER

*I refuse to allow any man-made differences to
separate me from any other human beings.*

Maya Angelou

We see this sign all the time: "Do not enter!" Other signs
have similar cautions.

"Under construction! Please excuse our mess."

"Caution! Enter at your own risk!"

A sign saying "Do not enter!"happened to be posted
on my seventeen-year-old son's bedroom door. I'm sure you

can figure out why. The funny thing is that the sign was not a deterrent to me. That sign was an invitation! I entered, yes, at great risk to my senses, yet willing to take that risk. It wasn't out of curiosity. It was out of sheer defiance.

After all, I am the mother.

And yes, I was horrified. Yes, I was not happy with what I found on the other side of the door (I'll spare you by not including a photo of the room). It's interesting to note that my unwanted inspection spurred on spring cleaning and the mess disappeared (yet the sign remained).

I think he believed he might as well keep the sign up because it was bound to get nasty in there again. And he hoped at some point I would stop caring about the mess on the other side of the door.

Some of us put the "Do not enter!" sign up as our default. Sometimes it's on our bedroom doors, and sometimes it's on our hearts. Initially, it draws attention, sort of like the morbid curiosity of driving by a car accident. We walk right into someone else's life, oftentimes uninvited, to see the mess on the other side of the door.

Our involvement or intervention may spur someone to clean up their act, but there is always that possibility that once we go back to our own lives, the dirty laundry will pile up again. After a while we stop caring because we don't understand why they just can't keep their stuff together. We're tempted to walk away.

I know my son just didn't feel that he could stay on top of things the way I expected him to. We all go through times when we don't have the energy to keep everything as it should be. We tape the "Do not enter!" sign on the door and honestly hope no one will see our mess. Even though my room is neat as a pin (at the moment), I can remember when, as a teen, it wasn't. My mother's answer was to close my bedroom door. She ignored my mess. But I can't ignore his mess. Not because I'm a neat freak, but because I know that how he handles today's mess affects how he'll handle tomorrow's mess. I want to be there to help him when he asks for it.

After all, I am the mother.

THOUGHT POKE

Are you organized and your child is, well, not? Are you good at math but your child isn't? Are you an introvert and your child is an extrovert? Recognize your differences, but understand that those differences affect how well you can help your child be who she is on her own. Remember that God will complete his good work.

> He who began a good work in you will
> carry it on to completion until the day of
> Christ Jesus. (Phil. 1:6)

———

CATCH AND RELEASE

Children should have enough freedom to be themselves—once they've learned the rules.

Anna Quindlen

At my waterside school the learning environment extends out to the end of our dock (and sometimes beyond). I was just getting to know these students, and I watched as something almost magical happened on dock day. Every classroom has behavior problems, and some have more than others. Some students struggle and seem to wrestle with the textbook. There are some students who just can't seem to keep still and wander around the room like lost puppies. These students, on dock day, were engaged, competent, focused, and literally joyous!

Maybe it was the fresh sea air; maybe it was getting out from behind those desks in the classroom. Whatever it was, it gave me a glimpse into the hearts of these budding teenagers, who showed me a side of themselves most teachers never see—that of confident and expert learners.

I marveled at the pixie who, with black nail polish, nose ring, and chains dangling from her hips, gathered a cast net back together and held one end in her teeth before throwing over the edge of the dock a perfect, wide circle into the waiting water. Moments later, she pulled the net up and counted her catch—about ten pinfish and one small blowfish! Just as expertly, she picked up each one and threw it back into the water. She knew from experience which were worth keeping and which weren't. Catch and release—that's how we do things on dock day.

We spend so much time trying to keep kids in a box of our making. Although the parameters are usually for their safety, I wonder how many of us say no more often than we say yes. Those things we say no to aren't always to keep our kids safe. They are for our convenience as parents and teachers. It seems easier to say no.

The problem is that the more we say no, the fewer opportunities our children will have to experience the world around them. Their strengths, their talents, their gifts may not show up until we say yes. We can let them experience the world and cast a wide net of experience. We don't have to accept everything they catch though. We can teach them how to identify what they catch in their nets as worth keeping or not—help them learn how to catch and release.

Maybe then we will learn how to catch and release as well.

THOUGHT POKE

Think about all those things you said no to today—can you change any to a yes tomorrow? Even if your children have the right to do anything, you are still allowed to remind them that not everything is beneficial.

"I have the right to do anything," you say—but not everything is beneficial. "I have the right to do anything"—but I will not be mastered by anything. (1 Cor. 6:12)

——

MOM, I BLEW
MY HEAD!

Freedom really means the freedom to make mistakes.

Ludwig von Mises, *Economic Policy*

Our younger son, Charles, was almost fifteen years old. He was a freshman in high school—the same high school I graduated from, I might add. First period started at 7:05 a.m., and he left the house to walk only a block to school while it was still dark.

In an attempt to encourage more independent behavior, no one got up with him in the morning. Those of you who know me aren't surprised that I don't get up at 6:15 a.m.—as I've said in the past to my "morning glory" friends, it's just plain wrong. All I know is that when I woke up, he was out the door and already halfway through first period. And that's a good thing.

High school was quite different than middle school was for Charles (and I would suspect for most kids). The expectations had easily tripled, and opportunities for activity abounded. Finding a way to get it all done was the challenge of each day. There was a lot of information for him to keep in his head, and since he wasn't in the habit of writing down what he needed to do (what would I do without my day planner?), he often forgot things. My fear was that he would forget to wake up in the morning!

Turns out, that wasn't worth worrying about. He got himself to school on time each day—in fact, on one particular morning he got there *early*.

He swears his alarm clock said 6:40 a.m. He panicked when he realized he had only a few minutes to get out the door and to school. He got up, dressed, made his bed, downed a breakfast shake, brushed his teeth, turned out the lights in the house, grabbed his backpack, and locked the front door on his way to meet his friends on the corner.

Boy, was it dark outside—darker than usual. And his friends weren't at the corner.

It was 3:50 a.m. And my son stood outside alone on a very dark corner, waiting for friends who were still slumbering.

Thankfully, he came right back into the house and went back to sleep (wish I could do that). He woke up on time a couple of hours later and still managed to get out the door and to school without waking anyone.

"I just blew my head," he said. "I don't know what I was thinking."

He wasn't thinking. Usually, that would annoy the heck out of me. But I realized something substantial. He was acting out of habit. He did everything he was supposed to do—just three hours earlier than he should. As frightful as it was for me to find out he was outside alone at that time of the morning, I was incredibly proud of how he responded to his "error."

He's not perfect. He's going to make mistakes, forget his homework, get up at the wrong time, and "blow his head." His dad and I are more concerned with how he reacts to those mistakes. Willingly admitting your mistake is something we should all aspire to do.

THOUGHT POKE

Encourage your kids to examine what they could do differently to avoid their particular mistakes. Learning from these mistakes now fosters a more successful future.

> Oh, that my steps might be steady,
> keeping to the course you set;
> Then I'd never have any regrets
> in comparing my life with
> your counsel.
> (Ps. 119:5–6 THE MESSAGE)

MY SON AND I DON'T WEAR THE SAME SIZE

*A man loves his sweetheart the most, his wife
the best, but his mother the longest.*

Irish Proverb

Our home had an open-door policy—our sons' friends were always welcome, and to be honest, I preferred having them hang out at our house. It gave me the opportunity to get to know their friends on a level I wouldn't have otherwise. Over the course of their teenage years and through the beginning of college, more than one of those friends came to live with us for a time. Our house became a haven for some and an escape for others. I'm not sure that was always a good thing. I found myself attached to their friends, and when they were gone, a part of me went with them.

Girlfriends were no different. We welcomed their companion choices and got to know them as if they were indeed the future daughters-in-law we hoped for. They were invited to dinner on a regular basis, they accompanied us on outings, and we watched their competitive natures during family game nights. I guess maybe we were trying them on—to see if they fit. One young lady in particular fit quite well. I will never forget Joanie and to this day miss her in our lives—well, my life, to be exact.

Joanie's mother and I were friends and faith partners. I remember the day we looked at one another and realized that if all went well, we might become more than that. We might become in-laws! Needless to say, we were excited at the prospect. The day my son and Joanie broke up, I cried. The future I'd envisioned fizzled like the bubbles in my ginger ale. It was flat and could not be resurrected.

My son knew who fit and who didn't in his life. I had come dangerously close to becoming one of those mothers who tried to wear her son's clothes. You've seen them—mother and son with matching outfits. Christopher knew who was right for him. Now it was a matter of whether his choice fit us. Or was it? I have to trust that our sons will make decisions based on what they know is best for them. Watching them try on those life-partner choices from outside the dressing room is not easy, but they're too old for me to go into the dressing room with them.

THOUGHT POKE

Tread carefully when your sons and daughters enter into relationships. Your opinion has the power to make them run toward or away from their future. You don't have to keep wise counsel to yourself; just give it and then trust your children to make the right choice for themselves.

> Plans fail for lack of counsel,
>   but with many advisers they
>   succeed. (Prov. 15:22)

POSITIVE EASE

But let your "Yes" be "Yes," and your "No," "No." For whatever is more than these is from the evil one.

Matthew 5:37 (NKJV)

I'm a knitter. For the first time, I learned how to make sweaters that actually fit and that people wanted to wear. This is no small feat. This, my friends, is a delicate dance between art and craft. I made sweaters for both of our sons for Christmas last year. They have different builds, and even though I measured carefully and knitted according to the prescribed pattern, when our younger son, Charles, tried his on, I could see how hard he was working not to disappoint me.

"It's good. Yeah, it's good. Well, it's good enough." He stumbled over these words like a drunk on a cobblestoned street. He kept shrugging his shoulders and pulling at the back of the neck. He wasn't confused; he was uncomfortable. For the introvert it's not always easy to express your wants and needs.

I snatched it back from him and with a smile asked, "How do you want it to fit? Like Under Armour, like a T-shirt, or like your hoodie?" If it didn't fit comfortably, he wasn't going to wear it. I made it so he would wear it. I needed to adjust the fit according to his specs, not the specs in the pattern I so carefully followed.

Getting Charles to tell me how he wanted his sweater to fit took several tries. It seemed that his desire to please and not disappoint me overshadowed his desire to have a sweater that actually fit. I came at it from a different direction. I noticed that he wore a favorite blue sweater several times a week. How that sweater fit him would tell me how he wanted this sweater to fit. It had enough room in it to wear over a shirt. The sleeves came down over his wrists. The bottom fell about two inches below his waist. Even with these new dimensions, I wasn't sure how much I needed to change my sweater to fit to him. So I took the blue one from him with the excuse of washing it and laid it out on a table. Placing my sweater atop his, I realized right away that I needed to add inches from top to bottom and side to side. That meant ripping out a lot of the work I'd already done, but I really wanted it to fit.

Weeks later, Charles tried on the sweater again. This time a smile crept to his lips, and I watched his whole body relax. That's all I needed. I didn't need his words to tell me that it now fit. I didn't need his accolades about what a talented knitter I was. I didn't need his thanks or his praise.

When we're comfortable, we tend not to say so. It's only when we're uncomfortable that we squirm and fuss and whine. Think about trying to put a toddler into a snowsuit. The toddler is an expert at letting you know what he wants and needs. It's not a mystery. He will let you know right away by telling you "No!"

Why is it that when we grow up, we defer to others about what works and what doesn't in our lives? Polite society aside, part of growing up means letting others know what is your "Yes" and what is your "No." I needed to let go of my design and provide more room in the pattern so my son could tell me what he needed.

THOUGHT POKE

Making adjustments when something doesn't fit is part of the job of letting go. Making room in your relationship so your kids can tell you, "No, that doesn't work for me," provides that positive ease.

> I have chosen the way of faithfulness;
>   I have set my heart on your laws.
> I hold fast to your statutes, LORD;
>   do not let me be put to shame.
>   (Ps. 119:30–31)

Day 29

———

SUNDAY BEST

*Maybe, now and then, we have to give up a
portion of our kingdoms—the things we hold
dearest—to find what it is God wants for us.*

Heather Blanton, *A Lady in Defiance*

You know how we get those reminders in the mail or
email? You know the ones: they're not always welcome,
but usually they're necessary. It's time for your pet's
heartworm test. It's time to renew your car registration.
It's time to renew your virus protection. It's time for your

teeth cleaning. When our sons went away to college, I wished they would get an automated "It's time to go to church" reminder. My own gentle reminders didn't seem to be making the impact I'd hoped they would.

"Did you check out the Catholic Student Center?" I asked.

"How about the Baptist Student Center?" I suggested.

"There's a student retreat coming up. Are you thinking about going?" I tried.

Finally, "Are you going to church this weekend?"

Crickets.

I have to admit I was a little disappointed that neither of our children made being part of a church family a priority in their now independent lives. They were always involved in church growing up. As a family we were all more than just present and accounted for—we served, we shared our time and talents, we learned, we loved, and we were loved. I couldn't understand why our boys didn't want that for themselves.

When they came home on weekends, we went to church as a family. That didn't always work though. I thought that going when they were home would be like making sure they took their vitamins—a way to make up for the fact that they didn't always eat right. Then again, they didn't take the vitamins I sent them back to school with either.

I worried that if they didn't go to church, they wouldn't have a strong foundation on which to stand as they battled the contrary beliefs and viewpoints they encountered. I worried that they would forget everything we'd taught them. I worried that this separation might be permanent. And okay, I admit, I worried that they were rejecting me if they rejected the church.

We're learning that the reason many church-attending young adults stop going to church upon graduating from high school has nothing to do with their families. Their faith just isn't personally meaningful to them. They do not have what we call "firsthand faith." The church has not become a valued expression in their lives—one that influences how they live and how they relate and how they grow. Church was something we wanted them to do. Even if they had good experiences growing up in a church, until they experience firsthand faith, it will always be their parents' faith.

Does this mean they will never return to church? Are my kids church dropouts? Maybe. Can I live with that? I have to. After all, it's not about our kids going to the church of Mom and Dad. It's about their journey to find their firsthand faith. I can hold on to my faith while my kids find their own. As long as they still like coming home for Sunday family dinners, I'm good.

THOUGHT POKE

Life and faith choices are about firsthand experiences. Are there ways you can let go of your kids long enough for them to experience for themselves what faith is all about? Remember, faith is the hope we have in what we cannot yet see.

> Faith is confidence in what we hope for
> and assurance about what we do not see.
> (Heb. 11:1)

Day 30

———

UNMASKED

See everything; overlook a great deal; correct a little.

Pope John XXIII

As parents we mediate many of our children's relationships during their early years. We help them form their first friendships, referee their sibling skirmishes, and explain that when their grandma's kisses come at them like the loud, rapid succession of machine-gun fire, it's because she loves them so very much! Be kind to your little sister. Respect your elders. Share with your friends. Children believe what we tell them about the people in their lives. After all, many believe in the tooth fairy, Santa Claus, and even the Great Pumpkin because we told them to.

Things change during the teen and young-adult years. This is the time when fantasy and reality diverge. Our natural instinct is to believe the best about people, and until you experience otherwise, it's the right way to go. When I was ten, I could explain away why my grandmother was too busy in the kitchen to sit down at the table and visit with us. After all, she'd prepared a huge Italian meal, and those dishes weren't going to wash themselves. When I was sixteen, I realized that what I believed about my grandmother was only partly true. She didn't sit at the table and visit with us, not because the dishes beckoned but because she couldn't be in the same room with my mother. I didn't know about their feud until I was much older. It was hidden from me behind the mask of forced lipsticked smiles and eating at the kids' table.

When our kids graduate to the grown-ups' table, they see and hear things about the people they love that they didn't know before. No amount of explanation or redirection can reposition the fallen masks of their aunts, uncles, grandparents, cousins—and yes, us, their parents. They see us for who we are. How they then choose to love us is up to them.

Just as my mother didn't want to taint my relationship with my grandmother by telling me all that was between them, I didn't want to tarnish the image my sons had of their relatives either. They loved their aunts, uncles, grandparents, and cousins. It was a beautiful thing! Once people we hold up on a pedestal begin to fall, it can be like Humpty Dumpty; we're unable to put all the pieces back together again.

My moment of letting go of the responsibility to shape my children's perceptions of their relatives came around the dining-room table during a normal Sunday extended-family dinner. I could have whisked the boys out of the room so their ears wouldn't hear the hate coming out of someone they loved. I could have protected them and extended their childlike relationship a little longer. But I didn't. I let it go, and I let it happen.

Seeing through the glass clearly for the first time can be disorienting and sometimes disturbing. I wanted my children to have an adult relationship with those they call family with their eyes wide open. They needed to learn that their relationships were not airbrushed like magazine covers. They needed to learn that love is a decision based on reality—warts and all. They can't unsee or unhear what happened at that dining-room table, but they can choose to love on their own terms—even if it's from a distance.

THOUGHT POKE

Remove the veil from your children's eyes. You may not be able to control what they then see, but you can show them how to love once the scales have fallen from their eyes.

> God demonstrates his own love for us in this: While we were still sinners, Christ died for us. (Rom. 5:8)

PICKY EATERS

Our lives are a sum total of the choices we have made.

Wayne Dyer

One common conversation among moms in my experience is whether or not, or to what extent, their children
are picky eaters. I will admit to feeling pretty happy with
the fact that our boys were not picky eaters. "They eat
what I cook or they go hungry!" I would report. After
all, I had no desire to become a short-order cook, and I
certainly didn't want to decide which restaurant to go to

based on whether they served chicken nuggets. It's been said that variety is the spice of life. Our kids learned to like spicy food before they were two years old. They ate a balanced diet; few, if any, processed foods; and a multivitamin every day from the time they were babies.

Is there something really wrong with either cooking separate meals for different kids or giving kids mac 'n cheese every night because that's all they will eat? I'm not here to start a fight—really, I'm not. What I've learned is that whether your kids eat only what you cook or only what they tell you they will eat, they are still being fed by food prepared by your hands. I love to cook, and cooking for my family is also an expression of love. Cooking certain foods or family favorites also carries on traditions that I got from my mother and grandmothers. It's all good until kids either go away to college or move out on their own. Cooking for your kids doesn't always make the list of things we need to let go.

The first time I visited our older son at college, I couldn't find a path to his room because of all the pizza boxes piled up around the suite. "We're recycling," he responded to the pained look on my face. "When?" I asked.

I discovered that he wasn't eating in the dining hall—due to his schedule, he claimed. I saw remnants of soda littering every available tabletop. "Are you eating well?" I knew the answer, but the Italian mother in me couldn't be contained. "Well enough" was all he said. When I saw the vitamins I'd sent with him were still unopened and in the plastic grocery-store bag, I just shook my head and kept quiet. After all, he was on his own now.

Three months later, our son came down with mono and shingles! He had to take incompletes in his courses and was miserable. The combination of a lackluster diet and college stress basically compromised his immune system, and this boy, who knew very well how to cook, found himself isolated in his room, weak and in pain. I couldn't understand how this could happen. What I learned is that even though he knew how to cook, he just didn't choose to cook for himself. He didn't make smart food choices on his own. I realized that I never gave him a chance to do that when he was at home. I chose.

Over Christmas break we worked on making smart food choices, and I made him responsible for meal planning for the whole family at least once a week. I stepped away and let go of my control over food. He made the menu, did the food shopping, and prepared the meal. He chose.

THOUGHT POKE

How often do your kids choose on their own what they will eat? Do they know how to choose wisely? Sometimes our children hold on to their childhoods and are slow to respond to the responsibilities of adulthood. Before you let go of this particular area of control, make sure they know how to choose wisely so they don't end up with scurvy!

> How long will you who are simple love
> your simple ways?
> How long will mockers delight in
> mockery
> and fools hate knowledge?
> (Prov. 1:22)

STORYTELLER

If you want your children to be intelligent, read them fairy tales. If you want them to be more intelligent, read them more fairy tales.

Often attributed to Albert Einstein

We read to our boys every night as part of their bedtime ritual. My husband, Chip, and I are both voracious readers, and as an educator I knew that reading with and to children is one of the keys to success in school. It started innocently enough. Dr. Seuss gave us one fish, two fish, and then some red and blue fish. Frog and Toad were definitely our friends. Eventually the children who lived in a boxcar won our hearts, and then we just couldn't get enough of those crazy kids in that magic tree house. Books filled the shelves in their bedroom. Stories easily captured their dreams. The library became their second home, and having it within walking distance was a gift.

Then this teenage wannabe wizard burst into our lives like the proverbial bull in the china closet. My mother gave Christopher his first copy of *Harry Potter and the Sorcerer's Stone*. She read it first and wrote a loving note to him on the inside cover. It's a gift he still cherishes. The bedtime ritual waned, and our boys began to choose their own books and read themselves to sleep. Well, it didn't usually put them to sleep. From what I understand from my sons many years later, they read late into the night— even on school nights!

One of the popular songs going around in our circles at the time was "Be Careful, Little Eyes, What You See." I thought I'd done a good job regulating what our kids saw, and, since you read with your eyes, what they read. I worried about the influence of the stories I didn't choose for them, the ones I didn't tell. Learning how to let go of controlling the media our children consumed was scary but oh so necessary.

Making decisions about the credibility and reliability of the stories they read and the stories other people tell is a critical act; it's an adult ability. To tell the difference between truth and fiction, you need to make comparisons. The choices are more than can fit on our children's pint-size bookshelves.

Different viewpoints, different genres, different voices all tell the stories of our lives. Focusing only on your own limited experience or those of a select few skews learning by someone else's bias. Allowing children to read widely provides them with a depth of understanding they might not otherwise gain from experience alone. We make better decisions when we are better informed. Encourage kids to read outside their areas of interest and knowledge. That's why for every Harry Potter book our son read, I asked that he read one of the hundred greatest books. The month he read *The Sorcerer's Stone*, he also read *The Call of the Wild*; when he read the third book in the *Lord of the Rings* trilogy, he also read *Great Expectations*.

Today, our older son is a teacher, and his reading preferences are still primarily fantasy and science fiction—but he also reads the works of Oliver Sacks, Friedrich Nietzsche, James Martin, and *The Onion*. I look at my bedside table and see a similar collection of voices. Funny how that happens.

THOUGHT POKE

Childlike innocence is for children. Let go of your power as the storyteller, and let your teens and young adults read on their own. How can you encourage them to read widely and travel extensively? What will it take for you to trust them to know the difference between fantasy and reality and not be taken captive by empty deceit?

> See to it that no one takes you captive through hollow and deceptive philosophy, which depends on human tradition and the elemental spiritual forces of this world rather than on Christ. (Col. 2:8)

———

HOMEWORK

*Even when we were with you, we would
give you this command: If anyone is not
willing to work, let him not eat.*

2 Thessalonians 3:10 (ESV)

When I was growing up, my parents didn't know how I was doing in school until I brought home my report card. I wasn't one of those kids who lost it or conveniently forgot to bring it home if there was bad news. I handed it over with the willingness of the girl who got caught with her hand in the cookie jar. I always struggled with something in school. I never got straight As. I worked really hard for every B. Fast-forward to college, where grades were easier to hide. Unless my parents asked to see them, I could easily hide my progress, or lack thereof, if I were so inclined. My school journey was mine alone to walk. It was up to me to do my homework, plan and execute a project, and ask for help when I needed it.

Things have changed.

The moment my sons' school district implemented the use of the online grade portal, I was hooked. I could check at any time of the day or night my kids' grades, their tardies or absences, outstanding homework assignments, and the like. As long as the teachers updated it, I was in the loop, never to be surprised again by my child's report card. Unfortunately, that loop became as tight as the embrace of a boa constrictor. It began to strangle my children's growing independence while it fed my desire for control. I found myself questioning the still-missing grades in the online portal when they arrived home. The after-school table talk accompanied by milk and cookies no longer revolved around the up-coming field trip to the history museum; it became an interrogation with a side of torture.

The online grade system was like a gateway drug for me. Before I knew it, I was leaving notes in teachers' mailboxes about the delays in their grade postings, and I found myself waiting late into the night for the grade to change by the eerie, greenish glow of the computer screen. What started out as being an engaged parent, a simple yet loyal foot soldier in this thing we call school, had quickly escalated into the control-addict behavior I'd always feared—the Black Hawk helicopter parent! Our younger son was the first to fall in this skirmish. The more I reminded him to do his homework, turn in completed work, study for his tests, and make up missed work, the less he did any of those things. He stopped any forward motion. He figured it out before I did—why walk on your own when someone's already pushing you?

I knew I had to quit. I knew this habit of mine was fostering a dependence I hadn't anticipated. Charles seemed to wait for me to tell him what to do for school.

I had, although inadvertently, squashed any sense of initiative or independent thinking a thirteen-year-old boy might possess. Mind you, I realize that the brain of a thirteen-year-old boy is in a state of flux—never quite sure what it should attend to—but I had made it almost impossible for him to take charge of his own learning. He didn't need to remember that he had an algebra test on Thursday because I reminded him. He didn't need to question a missing grade because I already did (even before he knew it was missing). He didn't need to remember because I was his memory.

Remember the saying "Give a man a fish and you feed him for a day. Teach a man to fish and you feed him for a lifetime"? Charles was eating fish every day—but I was afraid he was going to grow up hungry.

So I quit. No more online grade portal. No more notes to teachers. No more kitchen-table interrogations. It was time to teach my boy how to fish instead.

THOUGHT POKE

What are you doing for your kids that they could and should be doing for themselves?

> Teach me knowledge and good
> judgment,
> for I trust your commands.
> (Ps. 119:66)

Day 34

———

THE FALL OF "JUST YOU AND ME" DAYS

You can't start the next chapter of your life
if you keep re-reading the last one.

Author unknown

Thinking you've let go and then finding out "no, not quite, still holding on for dear life" is humbling. For the first time in my life, I went to visit our son and his wife in their new home. They were recently married and lived almost two thousand miles away from us—not my plan, but it is what it is. My excitement and longing to see my son trumped any forward thinking on my part. I should have considered what it would be like to sleep in my son's home and whether I would be comfortable and happy about that.

I wasn't comfortable.

The first hurdle was the fact that this was my son's home—not mine. This wasn't the temporary lodgings of a college dorm or the bohemian romance of his first apartment with his best buddies. This was his and his wife's place—a house, a newly established home. I was definitely a visitor—an interloper in their habitation. Although they prepared for my arrival by purchasing a new sleeper sofa (no dedicated guest room) and thought of my comfort by buying new sheets and ensuring the guest bathroom was squeaky clean, I laid awake that first night, shivering in the air-conditioning and fending off the advances of their cat.

The next hurdle, more difficult for me to clear, was the realization that I could not have my son to myself. In fact, after my short two days there, I felt as if I hadn't even seen him at all. When our boys were growing up, we established what I called "just you and me" days. I would set aside time, outings, or just space for me to be with each of my boys on his own. It was special. My boys and I treasured that time. I think my problem, which is a problem with expectations, was that I envisioned "just you and me" time with my son. I discovered I could no longer expect that. He was no longer "just you"—he was "Chris and Liz." I realized in that moment that my heart had not caught up with my head in realizing he was now married.

Managing our expectations is challenging as we learn to let our children go. Not only do we, the greatest and most supportive parents on the planet, have expectations, but so do our children. Most likely you've neither considered nor communicated them. The question is whether they *should* be communicated. Should I have let my son know that I expected to have dedicated time just with him? Or should I have let go of that expectation and then been giddy with surprise at the unexpected moments of "just you and me" if they came? Transitioning from making this about me to allowing it to be about him and his expectations was difficult. I haven't found my balance yet.

It's like having a hole punched in your inner ear—I'll be a little dizzy until it heals.

THOUGHT POKE

Experiencing frustration or disappointment with your children is often associated with either mismatched or unmet expectations. Can you articulate what your expectations are before you find yourself disappointed? Let yours decrease so theirs and the Lord's might increase.

> He must become greater; I must become less. (John 3:30)

BAGGAGE CLAIM

Doing what's right isn't the problem.
It is knowing what's right.
Lyndon B. Johnson

Two of our nieces traveled from Florida to New York on their own to visit us for part of the summer. At thirteen and sixteen these two made their way for the first time without parents. My sister had done a great job preparing them for this solo venture. Their itinerary was planned to the minute. I knew what time they left the house for the airport, when they checked in to get their unaccompanied-minor IDs, whether their luggage was checked or carried on, their flight number so I could track their progress online, and the name of the hostess from whom I would collect them at the Newark airport at exactly 12:45 p.m.

My sister texted me every step of her way with them. One of my nieces texted me every step of the rest of the way. The only time we didn't know where they were and what was happening was in midair when their phones were in airplane mode. It was an excruciating two hours. I watched the flight-status app on my phone track their flight with that little green line over Atlanta, then Charlotte, and then DC. At that point I left for the airport, which was an hour and a half away. I wanted to get there in plenty of time for their arrival. That was my only job—pick them up on time.

I didn't anticipate the traffic standstill on the thruway. I didn't anticipate my nieces' plane making great time and arriving early, and I didn't anticipate that my phone would die en route! Needless to say, I was thirty minutes late to the airport. My sister would kill me. My nieces would think their aunt didn't care enough to plan ahead—as their mother so lovingly did. I felt like a failure, a screwup, a nincompoop! I worried—would the hostess wait with them? I hoped they wouldn't talk to anyone—after all, this was their first trip to New York and there are crazy people here (now I sound like my grandmother). My heart was in my throat as we pulled up curbside at the arriving-flights area. I scanned the sidewalk for Kate's lithe form and Bree's blue-black hair. Nothing.

Then like magic, my phone chirped to life, announcing several unread texts.

> **Bree:** We landed early, Aunt Vicki. We'll meet you at baggage claim.

> **Bree:** We're at baggage claim. You must have run into traffic. We'll wait right here.

> **Bree:** The hostess left, but we're still here at baggage claim. Let me know when you're here.

I texted back while running into the terminal: "On my way. Stay there!" I looked up just in time to avoid running right into my niece, who was standing there at baggage claim with the biggest smile. Thirteen going on thirty, Bree hugged me and said, "I was so worried about you. Are you okay?"

Am *I* okay? She was worried about *me*. Right there, I put down the bags from my own growing up and how micromanaged I was by my parents and my grandparents. My sister did more than prepare her daughters' itinerary; she prepared them to handle the detours, delays, and derailments that may occur on their way. She also taught them a lesson for if you get lost or stranded—always meet at baggage claim.

THOUGHT POKE

The path set out before us may look straight, but it will come with bumps, holes, and roadblocks along the way. We don't need to dictate the path our kids will take on their journey, but we must teach them how to overcome the obstacles or how to choose an alternate route.

Worrying about what is ahead is not the way. How can you help prepare your child for the unexpected?

> "Martha, Martha," the Lord answered, "you are worried and upset about many things, but few things are needed—or indeed only one. Mary has chosen what is better, and it will not be taken away from her." (Luke 10:41–42)

Day 36

———

TWILIGHT TIME

Step back in perspective, open your heart and
welcome transition into a new phase of life.

Linda Rawson

The act of letting go of knowing everything going on in my children's lives was unfamiliar territory. As my kids grew up, so did I. It wasn't easy to get used to. I would sit up, waiting for them to come home after a night out with their friends. I hadn't downloaded that location app for their phones, so I had to worry the old-fashioned way—without GPS.

One specific time, I expected them by midnight. I sat near the kitchen, waiting for them. It was 12:05 a.m. My mind swirled around the coming consequences. Hopefully, I'd only need to give them a lecture. I'd have to remind them that it is unfair to worry their mother and that nothing good happens after midnight. Should I punish them? Should I take away their phones? What about the exposition of "as long as you live under my roof"? Maybe I should go to bed and not sit here, waiting like my grandmother did when I lived with her. She'd stand in the upstairs window, watching for my cab to pull up out front. Once she waited until 3:00 a.m. It wasn't a happy homecoming. Do I want to be *that* parent?

The clock now read 12:10.

They sauntered in at 12:15, laughing about something. They didn't even notice I was sitting there. I watched as they opened the fridge, scanning for something to eat. They sat down at the kitchen table and each ate a bowl of cereal. After they rinsed out their bowls and put them in the dishwasher, they locked the front door and headed to their rooms for the night. Still unseen, I turned out the kitchen light and went to bed. Chip squeezed my hand and whispered in the dark, "They're fine."

Did I explain that they were home from college? I'm glad they didn't see me waiting up for them. It allowed me to let go without an audience.

THOUGHT POKE

Try not to let your anxiety over letting go consume you; let it go so you can accept the rest already waiting for you.

> Come to me, all you who are weary and
> burdened, and I will give you rest. Take
> my yoke upon you and learn from me,
> for I am gentle and humble in heart,
> and you will find rest for your souls. For
> my yoke is easy and my burden is light.
> (Matt. 11:28–30)

HOT RODS

*How strange is this combination of proximity
and separation. That ground—seconds
away—thousands of miles away.*
Charles A. Lindbergh, *The Spirit of St. Louis*

Chip likes to remind the rest of us that he's been working since he was fifteen. "My first job was pumping gas,
and I've been working every day of my life since," he
explains with just a twinge of pride. My parents didn't

let me get a job until I went to college. "You'll be work-ing the rest of your life—no need to start now," they explained with just a twinge of regret.

There's a difference between wanting to work and needing to work when you're young. For many teens, working provides a sense of independence and pride—and some much-needed cash. After all, who is going to pay for that car, the gas that goes into that car, the insurance needed to cover the driver of that car, and the money needed to go out to the places they'll drive to in that car? We certainly couldn't. So our boys needed to work when they were teens. Both of our boys got their first jobs at fifteen. Sound familiar?

Learning how to manage money only happens when you have money to manage. The meager allowances we gave our kids just wouldn't cut it. When biweekly paychecks began to trickle in, the game changed. They opened bank accounts, created budgets, put away sav-ings, and had to make the hard choices: gas for the car or the new Nintendo game? There were times when the Nintendo game got the cash. Our kids would make mis-takes in their money management. I believe in natural consequences, but it's not always an easy thing to watch happen.

After saving for his red Camaro convertible for more than a year, our younger son bought his dream car. He was still in high school and working part-time, and we were proud of his ability to focus his savings in this way. Funny thing about cars: it costs something to buy one, and it costs something more to maintain one. You never stop paying once you own a car. We've learned this lesson over and over again ourselves. This is why I fantasize about walking to work and not needing a car. But I digress.

We graciously agreed to carry the insurance on his car, but he needed to pay for the gas and maintenance. This particular 1980s Camaro began to require regular visits to the mechanic. It lived in that garage more than it did in ours. Charles made some decisions on his own that we didn't know about until it was too late. Buy gas for the car to get to work or get the oil changed? He bought gas. It shouldn't have surprised anyone the day that car threw a rod and gave up the ghost. But Charles was surprised—shocked even. Now he had no car. Then he had no job because he had no car to get to the job. His independence took a backseat to his humility. He'd have to start over—which he did.

Starting over—even if it's over and over again—is what grown-ups do. Charles got a job that was within walking distance—I was so jealous—and began the arduous task of saving money to get another car and another chance at independence. I think it may be a good thing that we couldn't afford to fund his independence. We wouldn't have had a front-row seat to his eventual winning of this race if we had.

THOUGHT POKE

Just because you can afford to fund your children's lifestyle, should you? How can you give them opportunities to fly on their own before they actually leave the nest? They need to be able to count the cost for themselves.

> Suppose one of you wants to build a
> tower. Won't you first sit down and

estimate the cost to see if you have enough money to complete it? For if you lay the foundation and are not able to finish it, everyone who sees it will ridicule you, saying, "This person began to build and wasn't able to finish." (Luke 14:28–30)

TELLING THE TRUTH IN LOVE

Speaking the truth in love, we will grow to become in every respect the mature body of him who is the head, that is, Christ.

Ephesians 4:15

Pride and Prejudice is one of my favorite books—I'm a romantic, so no surprise there. Every time I read it, I gain at least one more life lesson. This time around, I held my breath as Elizabeth Bennet admits to her father that she no longer dislikes Mr. Darcy and that she was wrong about him all along and now loves him like crazy. Her father, wanting only her happiness, giggles at her admission and gives her his blessing.

I've watched my sons fall in and out of love over the years. They always start out quite sure about the girl and their own feelings. They are steadfast and loyal to a fault. I say loyal to a fault because they believe in commitment so much that even if they realize she's not the one, they stay. Sometimes they stay too long. Finding out you're wrong about someone to whom you've given your heart is not an easy thing to accept. Admitting it to your parents, who may have known all along that it wasn't meant to be, is heroic.

I listened patiently as our younger son unveiled his heartache: He didn't love her. He hadn't loved her in a long time. He thought he'd feel better. He kept waiting to feel better. The wait lasted more than a year. He needed to tell her, and he knew once he did, it would be over. She would be hurt. He doesn't like hurting people. He was wrong. She wasn't the one. I think he wanted my blessing to let the relationship go. He'd bought a ring, after all—nonrefundable.

I gave him my blessing. I, just like Mr. Bennet with his Elizabeth, wanted him to be happy. I wanted him to be sure. He was the one who had to be sure. It wasn't and isn't about me. I had prayed for clarity for him all the way through that three-year relationship. That's all I could do. I could have raised red flags (there were a few). I could have suggested they weren't the best fit (*suggested* is a euphemism for sticking my nose in where it's not wanted, if you couldn't tell). I did none of those things; I didn't want to alienate my son.

When it was time, he came to me. When it was time, he spoke the truth. When it was time, he did what was called for and swallowed his pride. Better that than swallowing vows he couldn't keep.

THOUGHT POKE

Elizabeth Bennet felt safe enough to approach her father and tell him the truth of her heart. Have you given your kids enough space in their decision making to admit when they are wrong?

> May these words of my mouth and this
> meditation of my heart
> be pleasing in your sight,
> LORD, my Rock and my Redeemer.
> (Ps. 19:14)

NEVERLAND

*Listen to counsel and accept
discipline, that you may be
wise the rest of your days.*
Proverbs 19:20 (NASB)

I marvel at Lydia and her adventurous spirit. As much as her parents didn't want her to go, she went away to college, albeit only three hours away. As much as her parents protested, she then went overseas to work as an international hostess at a hotel in Austria after college.

This was not her major, by the way. The initiative and perseverance it takes to do what you believe you are meant to do, even when your parents aren't 100 percent behind you, is breathtaking. Some of us don't venture beyond our own backyards. We make our homes so comfortable for our kids that they have no real reason to go. That used to be called "failure to launch." Now it's called the "gap year."

The media reports that for the first time in 130 years, more young adults in the United States live with their parents than with a spouse or partner.[1] Moving out on your own used to be a rite of passage, a badge of honor. Now it's the least attractive life experience. We can blame the economy, the ridiculous amount of student-loan debt our kids may have accrued, or the frustrating housing market for this devolution of the young adult. Those

---

1   Richard Fry, "For First Time in Modern Era, Living with Parents Edges Out Other Living Arrangements for 18- to 34-Year-Olds," *Pew Research Center*, May 24, 2016, www.pewsocialtrends.org /2016/05/24/for-first-time-in-modern-era-living-with-parents -edges-out-other-living-arrangements-for-18-to-34-year-olds.

realities of the twenty-first century negatively affect a life independent of Mom and Dad, to be sure. But I suspect there is more to it than that.

Many recent grads are taking a gap year after either high school or college. They're taking time to travel or volunteer or explore other interests before settling down into the full responsibilities of real adult life. Hailed as a way for our kids to be more mature and better prepared for the next step in their young lives, the gap year has gained momentum among millennials. However, there is a downside to this gap that is rarely acknowledged. Although domestic and international programs exist that cost very little and provide housing to those who seek them, the skills needed to prepare for life on your own are missing. If everything is covered, like an all-inclusive cruise, how do you know how much life really costs? In addition, one gap year can easily turn into two or, in the case of our friend Jeremy, four! Out of college for four years, Jeremy has jumped from one gap assignment to the next. He may never come home. He may never grow up. It's like living in Neverland!

It's funny how when I was growing up, many of my peers wanted to take a break after high school or college and backpack across Europe. That was rarely welcome news to any parent. Delaying the inevitable is not always a good thing. As much as I admire Lydia for her worldwide adventures and am just a smidge jealous, at twenty-five she's back stateside, living with her parents, without a clue about what to do next. Wendy may have loved flying around with Peter Pan, but down deep, she knew growing up was what she really needed and wanted to do. If your child is delaying the inevitable, go ahead and offer that wise counsel. Even when fully grown, they still need to hear the truth in love.

THOUGHT POKE

There's a balance between letting our kids make their own decisions and cautioning them with our wise counsel. As much as we want our kids to have great life experiences, eventually it's time for them to grow up. Have you made your nest too comfortable? Or are you supporting them in ways that aren't healthy?

My mouth will speak words of wisdom;
the meditation of my heart will
give you understanding.
(Ps. 49:3)

PLAYING THE LONG GAME

Failures, repeated failures, are finger posts on the road to achievement. … One fails forward toward success.

Often attributed to C. S. Lewis

My father taught me how to play golf when I was quite young. I wasn't half bad, but I wasn't half good either. Dad had to remind me that even though I was adept at putting, what mattered more was being better able to play the long game—hitting those long drives consistently. My putting game wouldn't matter if I couldn't even get on the green. I've learned that golfers aren't the only ones who have to learn how to play the long game.

"He hates me," Chris finally blurted out after the longest silence on record. The best conversations always seem to happen in the car ride home from school.

I remember when I met Mr. Hayden at the open house in October. I could tell he was a no-nonsense, business-only type of teacher. There would be no nurturing of my son's gifts and talents during chemistry this year. I think Chris had finally met his match in Mr. Hayden, and he didn't appreciate it one bit.

"Well, he doesn't know how to teach," he protested. "He expects us to basically teach ourselves. He never explains anything. How am I supposed to learn in that class?"

I had never seen my son so frustrated over school. For the first time he was hitting a wall and couldn't figure out how to get over it.

"I want to transfer to another class," he said. "I hear Mr. Sterling actually teaches in his section of the class. I can't afford low grades, Mom. Why can't he just follow the book?"

"Did you go through the online tutorial Mr. Hayden provides? He explained that to us during open house," I gingerly suggested.

"I don't want to have to work that hard," he finally admitted. "Too many Cs and I won't get that scholarship."

There it was. What I always knew but he'd never admitted—Christopher didn't want to work that hard. He'd never had to before. He didn't know how. Well, that's a problem. There was way too much of his life in front of him to give up now. I could see it as if we were in a movie that overused the flash-forward cinematic storytelling technique. The sepia-soaked scene depicted our older son still needing me to run interference for him well into his thirties. Smoothing out every bump and making sure of every jot and tittle became my job and not his. He was living an airbrushed life!

Our son is talented and gifted in many ways. But it was time he learned how to play the long game. The only role I wanted to play now was that of his caddie. He had all the right clubs in his bag; he just needed to use the ones I suggested to the best of his ability.

"You have two great resources at your disposal, my dear. Use the online tutorial and your teacher. Ask him for help. That's music to any teacher's ears," I reminded. "Your success or failure is up to you."

He eked out a C+. He got his scholarship, went to college, and dealt with difficult professors for the next four years. The only difference then was that he knew what clubs he needed to drive the ball forward and onto the green. He didn't need me to caddie for him anymore.

THOUGHT POKE

Do you find yourself intervening to protect your children from disappointment or failure? Learning from our mistakes is a time-honored way to grow. Let your kids get acquainted with responsibility, self-discipline, and respect for authority. It's part of the long game.

> No discipline seems pleasant at the time, but painful. Later on, however, it produces a harvest of righteousness and peace for those who have been trained by it. (Heb. 12:11)

DRIVING MISS DAISY

*Each child is an adventure into a better life—an
opportunity to change the old pattern and make it new.*
Hubert H. Humphrey

Getting around on your own has long been considered
an adult ability. For many of my generation, getting
your driver's license at age sixteen was the first of many
steps on the journey to being on your own. I grew up
in a place where public transportation was how we all
got around, including getting to school, but we moved

to the suburbs when I was a teenager. Suddenly my independence options became quite limited. Getting my driver's license at sixteen was as important to my survival as breathing.

That's why it's difficult to grasp why so many teens are now opting out of getting their driver's licenses. It would be fine if that just meant they are choosing public transportation instead or getting around on their own power—like riding a bike or walking—but it seems that Mom's chauffeur days don't end when kids graduate from high school. Diana couldn't meet her husband for their anniversary dinner because she was driving their twenty-year-old son to his six-month dental-cleaning appointment—an appointment she made for him—and picking him up from an apartment she pays for. Dylan, her son, doesn't drive. He doesn't want the hassle of it, he says. Needless to say, her husband was not amused.

Driving *is* a hassle. So are the car and insurance payments, gas, and those pesky oil changes. It's okay to ditch driving; many people do. No reliable public transportation in your area? Some buses only get you from mall to mall. Not within walking distance to school or work? Is your Schwinn a little rusty? Getting around on your own is a problem to solve. Mom should not always be the solution. It's important that our kids can get themselves where they need to go when they need to get there. Inevitably, they will find themselves somewhere they don't want to be at a time they shouldn't be there with people they no longer want to be around. Instead of calling Mom in the middle of the night, which is every parent's nightmare, they should find their own way home. Remember, that's what Uber is for.

And by the way, just because they have a driver's license doesn't ensure they'll go to the dentist. My boys seem to avoid that particular destination.

THOUGHT POKE

The lure of the open road is not enough to entice some to get out on their own. Have we squashed our kids' thirst for adventure, and therefore independence, by always being the one to take them where they want to go?

Forget the former things;
>   do not dwell on the past.
See, I am doing a new thing!
>   Now it springs up; do you not
>   perceive it?
I am making a way in the wilderness
>   and streams in the wasteland.
>   (Isa. 43:18–19)

SLEEPING GIANT

Some people believe holding on and hanging in
there are signs of great strength. However, there
are times when it takes much more strength
to know when to let go and then do it.

Ann Landers

When I'm having a particularly disappointing or stress-
filled day, well-meaning friends post puppy pics or videos
in hopes of making me smile and forget for the moment the ache in my heart. Puppy pics work for me, but

precious sleeping babies are fast becoming what make me swoon. I never used to be *that* mom; babies were cute, but truly, only *my* babies were cute—other people's, well, they were okay. Now that our children are grown, a different biological clock has begun to tick, and I'm longing for babies again. It seems I have two hearts—who knew?

But here's the thing—I didn't even know this longing was inside me. Looking back, I now understand why my own mother was indignant when I told her that at fifty she would become a grandmother. Too soon. Too young. I also never understood why my friends whose children were having children decided they needed a bigger house—when the rest of us couldn't wait to downsize—in anticipation of family visits with grandbabies in tow.

Over the years my Grinch-like outlook toward grandchildren has changed—my heart has grown three sizes. My heart doesn't feel so tight, so limiting. In fact, it's bursting! It's as if a sleeping giant has been awoken—watch out, world! I'm ready—so why aren't they?

The decision to have children is just that for many people—a decision. What happens when your children choose not to have children? Or what happens if they can't? Or if they seem to be waiting forever? It doesn't matter if I'm finally ready. It no longer matters what they will call me—Nana, Nonnie, Grandma, Grammie. Since I couldn't decide, did I somehow jinx it? And in that moment of knowing that the future won't include a bigger house with lots of guest rooms, does it matter that the heart that grew three sizes is now broken?

It does matter—since the decisions family members make often affect every member of that family. Yet each couple must be given the grace to make their own decisions, and I need the grace to be able to rejoice with them when they rejoice and mourn with them when they mourn. *With* them—not apart from them.

My daughter-in-law sent me a picture the other day that did make me smile and, for a moment, swoon—my son, asleep, with their puppy.

THOUGHT POKE

Is your heart broken over a life decision your child has made? We cannot burden our children with our unrealized dreams or image of our future selves. Can you find the grace to love and support them whether or not what matters to you matters to them?

> This is my prayer: that your love may abound more and more in knowledge and depth of insight, so that you may be able to discern what is best and may be pure and blameless for the day of Christ. (Phil. 1:9–10)

———

BOOT-CAMP BASICS

With self-discipline most anything is possible.

Theodore Roosevelt

The beauty of social media is that you can witness the lives of people you know or once knew in ways you never would otherwise. As a teacher I've often wondered if some of my most troubled students even made it out of adolescence. They were the ones I worried about and had recurrent nightmares about; they were the ones with the deck stacked against them. For one young man, who made my life as his teacher torturous when he was in sixth grade, his future turned out so much more than expected—by anyone. Because of Facebook I had a front-row seat to his success.

Peter had a problem with impulse control. A highly gifted student, he just didn't know how to prioritize. It was more than always attending to the urgent over the important; it was attending to everything over the important. His parents were at a loss. He had to repeat sixth grade, and the last time I saw him, it was questionable if he would make it out of middle school. The crazy part was that Peter was lovely to be around. He had a great spirit and a tender heart. When I heard his parents sent him to military school, I had mixed feelings. I knew he needed to learn self-discipline, but I hoped the experience wouldn't crush his spirit.

Peter graduated from high school. I saw photos of him in his dress uniform with a beautiful young lady by his side. He looked so happy, with this perfect blend of confidence, security, and joy. I reached out to him in the usual way—through a private message—to congratulate him and to ask a question: "Did military school give you what you needed?"

Military school is like four years of boot camp. There's a lot to learn in boot camp. "It was exactly what I needed," Peter began. "I've got my priorities straight now. I know what's important and what's not."

In boot camp soldiers learn that their lives are broken down into two piles: things you want to do (sleep, read or write mail, talk with your buddies) and things you have to do (shine your shoes, roll your laundry, buff floors, scrub toilets). The temptation will be strong to slack off and procrastinate. First piece of advice—don't. Take care of what you have to first. Military school didn't make Peter disciplined—but it set up an environment in which he could learn self-discipline.

That self-discipline can be fostered, not necessarily taught. As adults, we may still be learning it. I know for myself that my life is broken down into two piles: things I want to do (knit, read, travel, visit with friends) and things I have to do (work, fold laundry, cook, walk the dog). Believe me, I think about it every day while teaching, while grocery shopping, while grading—I get to knit soon! We all have to learn the importance of eating our vegetables before having dessert. Peter learned—at military school.

THOUGHT POKE

Is your home environment set up to foster self-discipline? Without it our children walk through life unprotected. Learning how to focus on what's important is part of letting go of what's not.

> Like a city whose walls are broken
> through
> is a person who lacks self-control.
> (Prov. 25:28)

Day 44

NEARSIGHTEDNESS

Those who know your name trust in you, for you,
Lᴏʀᴅ, have never forsaken those who seek you.

Psalm 9:10

Kids tend to be nearsighted. At least mine were—they both wore glasses. But what I really mean to say is that kids can't see far. They live in the moment, the today, the right now. It's a developmental truth. This makes things challenging for us as we encourage them to think before they act and engage in long-term planning. They just don't realize how what they do today affects what happens in their lives tomorrow. And it is so easy for us to take control of the now so things will work out for our kids later.

Senior year in high school has become about applying to get into a good college. Junior year has become about preparing to apply to get into a good college. There are entire books written about planning for college—yes, even a book for dummies. Our older son is no dummy, but planning for college challenged his sight like the smallest letters on the eye chart.

The thing is—nearsightedness is hereditary. I'm nearsighted too. I struggled with seeing far. Would he make the same mistakes I did?

Although he was highly qualified, the number of colleges he would apply to depended on how many essays he was willing to write. He applied to a total of two colleges. Two. I was surrounded by moms who were creating entire spreadsheets to monitor their child's college applications. Christopher's peers were applying, on average, to seven to ten colleges. They were shooting for the moon! He was quite comfortable just standing on our roof.

I worried that his lackadaisical approach to planning for college would position him for a disappointing future. We want the best for our kids; we want them to succeed. When it came down to it, what I really wanted was for each of my kids to be happy with his choices. Would Christopher regret not applying to Duke or MIT or Yale? Would he feel trapped in mediocrity by going to a college close to home? Would he always wonder what would have happened if he'd just written more essays? I discovered at his graduation that those questions were mine alone. He hadn't wondered about any of those things.

Now as a working adult, married and living in his own home, I see a man who knows who he is and what he wants and who takes all the right steps to get where he wants to go. It's a developmental truth at this stage. My worries were my worries. I'm relieved that I didn't make them his. He's figured it out. He may still be nearsighted, but now that he wears corrective lenses, he can see far.

THOUGHT POKE

Trusting and hoping for our kids' future is challenging. It's difficult to see accurately what lies ahead. That trust can correct your own nearsightedness. Put on the glasses of trust. Can you ask yourself first if the future you are trusting for is your own or theirs?

> Trust in the LORD with all your heart
> and lean not on your own
> understanding;
> in all your ways submit to him,
> and he will make your paths
> straight. (Prov. 3:5–6)

CAMP WANNABEGONE

*I think sometimes parents and teachers fail to stretch
kids. My mother had a very good sense of how to
stretch me just slightly outside my comfort zone.*

Temple Grandin

You'd think we'd dropped them off on a desert island
with no food or supplies and no hope of rescue. The
looks on our boys' faces when they realized, too late,
that they really didn't want to go to sleepaway camp

after all almost broke my heart—almost. My husband and I were looking forward to one week without kids. We realized that after thirteen years of being parents, we hadn't been separated from our kids for more than a day. We all needed to learn how to get along away from one another. The comforts of home were stripped away, and our boys would have to just deal with it. That's a good life lesson, right? Just deal with it!

They were only fifteen miles away, but they were sleeping in cabins with bunkmates, and they weren't together. The showers were outside, there was no air-conditioning, and they had to share a bathroom with six other boys. We were told by the camp director that they could call home or we could call them only once during their week away. As anxious as I was to hear their voices and know they were okay, I thought it was better if we waited until close to the end of the week to contact them. Maybe by then they wouldn't have as much to complain about.

Saturday came and went, and I realized as I dropped off to sleep that we hadn't called the boys the entire week! I guess Chip and I were having too good of a time and forgot we had kids (not really). When we picked them up the next morning, I was ready for two sulky boys who felt abandoned and forgotten. What we found instead was one boy with bandages on both knees and one still shaking from a fright in the dark woods the night before. Overall, they'd had a good time. It turned out that it wasn't that they missed us or the trappings of their own home so much as they were challenged by trying something totally new and out of their comfort zones.

"I liked camp," Charles said. "I could go again."

"I liked camp," Christopher said. "But I never want to go again."

It's so tempting to stick to the familiar and the status quo. Like plants, kids don't grow well under glass. They need new surroundings, a little stress from uncertainty, and the chance to bloom like wildflowers instead of award-winning roses. Learning to adapt to new surroundings makes you stronger and more sure of yourself. After all, strong trees bend in the wind; their roots grow deeper. We can give our kids deeper roots if we don't protect them so much from the wind.

THOUGHT POKE

Is it windy where you live, or is there not even a hint of a ripple in the atmosphere? Find ways to shake it up a bit and let go of the climate control so your kids can stand tall on their own.

> Blessed is the one who trusts in the
>> LORD,
>>> whose confidence is in him.
> They will be like a tree planted by the
>> water
>>> that sends out its roots by the
>>>> stream.
> It does not fear when heat comes;
>> its leaves are always green.
> It has no worries in a year of drought
>> and never fails to bear fruit.
>>> (Jer. 17:7–8)

———

SEEKING A SECOND OPINION

The way of a fool is right in his own eyes,
but a wise man listens to advice.

Proverbs 12:15 (ESV)

What we choose to share on social media reflects only what we are willing to put out there for both public consumption and public opinion. That "like" button can be a powerful motivator or deterrent for those who are reliant on others' opinions to make decisions. But how often do our kids put their lives out there for review? When they're looking for validation, more than you think. Our kids have gone well beyond seeking their parents' approval of their plans. In fact, many kids bypass it altogether. They've opened their choices up to the court of public opinion instead.

> **Post:** "Staying in bed and blowing off work. Feeling too tired to be responsible today."

> **Likes:** 230

> **Comments:**
> "Be good to yourself. Take time to rest."
>   —Shannon
> "Go back to bed, Ferris!" —Justin
> "Make sure you stay off-line if you stay
>   home." —Caitie
> "Text me!" —Jake
> "Text me!!!" —Mom

Char, already at work, was just grateful she could see the posts; otherwise, she wouldn't have known her darling daughter wasn't going to work that day. At college and more than five hundred miles away, Jillian doesn't usually check with her mom about her day-to-day choices. With 230 likes and positive comments from her peers, she probably felt pretty good about her decision to stay home. After all, majority rules.

Does this mean Char should stay out of it and let her daughter live with whatever consequences come with calling off work with little to no notice? This is tricky territory. Letting go is the goal, but sometimes the tie that binds isn't a tether but a lifeline. Just because your child doesn't seek a second opinion—yours—doesn't mean you can't offer one. She will still make her own decision, but at least it will be an informed decision.

Char picked up the phone and called her daughter. She was surprised when she actually answered (doesn't usually happen). "Thought I'd check in on you," she began. "I heard you weren't feeling well. Just remember that people are counting on you to cover your shift today.

Make sure you don't leave them hanging. No one likes to be left hanging. It's never appreciated."

There. Now whatever Jillian chose to do, she did knowing the full impact of that choice. Two hundred and thirty likes aside, sometimes it takes just one voice to turn the tide. Char let go and went back to work. After all, she didn't want to leave them hanging either.

THOUGHT POKE

Offering a second opinion when unsolicited can be like walking into murky water. You can't see what you're stepping into. Just be prepared to let go of the decision making after you offer that opinion. When was the last time you inserted your opinion even when you weren't sure it would be welcome?

> Let the wise listen and add to their
> learning,
> and let the discerning get guidance.
> (Prov. 1:5)

OUT OF SIGHT, OUT OF YOUR MIND!

When I was a child, I spoke like a child, I thought like a child, I reasoned like a child. When I became a man, I gave up childish ways.

1 Corinthians 13:11 (ESV)

Giving kids their own space introduces one degree of separation between parent and child. They move from the cradle in your bedroom (or your bed if you were so inclined) to their own room. Our boys shared a room until they were ten and eleven years old. Then we separated them, and like separating conjoined twins, it was a little problematic at first. Our younger son didn't like sleeping alone. He felt abandoned by his big brother, who had moved into his own room in the basement. Our older son, on the other hand, loved his new life in his own space (albeit a little creepy down there for my taste).

One problem with being separated by an entire floor? Parental blindness.

"Use your brain!" I heard Chip say to our older son, who was standing, still dripping wet, in the kitchen. Confused as to why Christopher was still wet when his bathroom was downstairs in his newly separate living suite, I looked closely and realized he still had shampoo in his hair as well.

"Why do you still have shampoo in your hair?" Now I wondered if there was something wrong with the shower.

"It's not shampoo," he started. "It's soap. I'm out of shampoo."

"How long have you been out of shampoo?" My husband's face showed how baffled he was by this apparent lack of common sense.

"I don't know. Maybe a couple of weeks."

Thoughts?

Mine included wondering what else was not quite right downstairs, wrestling with being angry or laughing uncontrollably, and then asking myself whether we had jumped the gun on this trial separation. After what felt like an hour of shocked silence (though in reality my husband didn't miss a beat), Chip said, "So, next time, what do you think you need to do when you run out of shampoo?"

"Tell you?" Christopher ventured a guess.

"That's a start. Any other ideas?"

"Um, put it on the shopping list?" Now the wheels were turning.

"Anything else?" Chip queried.

"Check before I get into the shower?" Christopher lit up with understanding. "Get some from your bathroom?"

As our son pounded down the stairs two at a time with a new shampoo bottle in hand, I knew he wouldn't make that mistake again. In fact, being one floor away was practice for what was to come—being two thousand miles away. I admit I sit here today and still wonder if he has thought of everything he needs to be out there on his own. Did he get the oil changed in his car? Did he pay his phone bill? Did he file his taxes? He may be out of my sight, but he's never off my mind.

THOUGHT POKE

How are you physically separated from your children at this point? Whether it's one room away or miles away, part of being separate is being mindful. Cultivate critical thinking now so they can think for themselves later.

> Now we see in a mirror dimly, but then
> face to face. Now I know in part; then I
> shall know fully, even as I have been fully
> known. (1 Cor. 13:12 ESV)

THE LAUNCH CYCLE

If you want children to keep their feet on the ground,
put some responsibility on their shoulders.

Abigail Van Buren

When I read *The Martian*, I couldn't help but notice that as I read, I was problem-solving right along with the main character, who found himself stranded on Mars with no realistic hope of rescue. I'm not an engineer, nor am I technically minded by any stretch of the imagination, but I recognized the power of creative thinking when I saw it played out through the adventures and misadventures of Mark Watney up there on Mars. Thinking through a problem, brainstorming possible solutions, trying out solutions, and evaluating how well they worked are all steps taken in the creative problem-solving process. This process is born out of struggle and matured through risk and uncertainty—two things we tend to shield our kids from.

One of the most poignant moments for me in *The Martian* was noticing how important it was to work well together as a team when facing a seemingly insurmountable problem. Launch teams operate this way from the conception of the mission to the landing of the spacecraft. The interesting thing is that if you find yourself stranded and alone, you no longer have a team to help you solve the survival problem; you have to do it by yourself. If God wills, you will rely on all that you learned while working in a team to get by. But circumstances may not be the same as they were when you were together, and you might have to improvise.

Our family is a team. Chip and I grew as parents and adults right alongside our boys as they grew into men. We faced the challenges of growing up together. The skills our children learned while being part of this team have served them well as they've walked out in the waiting world. But there were and continue to be problems for them to solve as they become mission ready and able to launch.

When our older son decided he'd rather live off campus than in the dorms at college, I wasn't convinced this was a risk worth taking. I had a long list of reasons why it was preferable that he stay on campus, but at twenty years old Christopher knew what he wanted to do and did it. At this point his finances were completely in his hands; we no longer supported him. There were no financial strings to tie us together, so I had no leverage in the decision making.

As I look back, I see that our son did a great job navigating the problems that arose from getting an apartment while still in college. There were times when we were in contact to be his sounding board while he was struggling for solutions, but overall, he figured it out himself in sometimes quite creative ways. Having three roommates turned out to be the way to go, for instance. Now I'm watching from a distance (from New York to

Colorado) as he navigates buying his first home. He knows his "team" is ready and within communication distance to help him solve this grown-up challenge, but he hasn't engaged our help—yet. The letting go that occurred while he was in college has made him a stronger and more capable adult in the present. Mission control will always be there if he needs it, but ultimately, he has to pilot his craft on his own.

THOUGHT POKE

Sooner rather than later, your kids will be out of communication range and will have to make decisions on their own. How can you give them simulation opportunities so they will know exactly what to do without you?

> Whatever you have learned or received
> or heard from me, or seen in me—put it
> into practice. And the God of peace will
> be with you. (Phil. 4:9)

———

IT'S THE CLIMB

Whoever wants to reach a distant goal
must take many small steps.

Helmut Schmidt

The Manitou Incline is a two-thousand-foot almost-vertical hike up part of Pikes Peak in Colorado. It is considered an extreme hike for even the most accomplished athlete. I've never climbed it, nor do I expect I ever will. Many of my friends have, and I see their posts about reaching the top in one piece. But not everyone has been so lucky.

Accounts of deaths on the Incline are not unheard of; you climb at your own risk.

When our younger son announced he was going to do the Incline the next morning, his young twenty-year-old life flashed before my eyes. He assured me he wasn't going alone; a family friend and experienced climber was going with him.

"Come with me," Charles invited.

Then *my* life flashed before my eyes!

Oh, how I wanted to climb the Incline with my son. It's a rare thing for your college-age child to include you in anything, but I would have slowed him down at best or stopped his ascent at the very worst because I wasn't prepared to make such a trip.

"I've been training," he explained in answer to the pained look on my face. "I can do this."

"Let me know when you get to the top, okay?" I requested. "Don't take any pics until you reach the top. I don't want you distracted along the way."

The next morning I was on my knees in prayer for the next two or three hours—praying about what it takes to climb those old, abandoned rail ties on the side of

America's Mountain. All the last-minute pieces of advice I'd given Charles replayed in my mind: stay hydrated, don't look down, stop when you need to, take your time, and let me know when you're there safe and sound.

At noon my phone chirped, and in came a pic of a weary but oh-so-proud young man. He stood at what looked like the edge of a cliff (as if I needed more to worry about) with the whole of Colorado Springs spread out below him. He was on top of the world! All I could do now was wait for him to descend.

As he relayed the harrowing tale of the climb, Charles was more alive than I'd seen him in many months. From the story of the false summit to the fact that he had thrown up only once by the time he reached the top, this boy of ours connected to his potential in a way I could never have provided for him. He didn't need me to be his cheerleader. He didn't need me to be his chaperone. He didn't even need my permission. He just needed me to let him take this step (or 2,700 steps in this case) on his own.

It was kind of my son to invite me to join him on his journey. But I was content to stay on the ground while he made his climb.

THOUGHT POKE

Our kids will go some places where we can't accompany them. Let them go it alone; let their journey be their own. What parts of their journey are driving you to your knees? Believe it or not, that's a great place to be!

> Do not be anxious about anything, but in every situation, by prayer and petition, with thanksgiving, present your requests to God. And the peace of God, which transcends all understanding, will guard your hearts and your minds in Christ Jesus. (Phil. 4:6–7)

DON'T WORRY;
BE HAPPY

Brothers and sisters, stop thinking like children. In regard to evil be infants, but in your thinking be adults.

1 Corinthians 14:20

After several changes to his chosen major in college, our older son finally graduated with a degree in biology. His transition to the working world was not as easy as expected. He knew what he *didn't* want to do—work in a lab isolated from others—but he truly could not put a finger on what it was he *did* want to do. What does it mean to be a biologist anyway? He didn't want to work out in the field. He didn't want to go premed. He didn't want to continue in the sciences for his master's degree. Knowing what you do want is sometimes so much harder.

It's not that Christopher wasn't capable of taking any of the above-mentioned biology-related paths. More than capable, yet unwilling. Caught up in the myth that whatever you do, make sure it makes you happy, he was paralyzed to move forward. I think I was partly to blame for this paralysis. I told him over the course of his growing up that it didn't matter what he did in this life as long as he loved what he did. This pronouncement was born out of watching my own father work a job he hated for forty years. He made sure I knew that being happy in your work is important. And I was and am happy in my work. Now this same advice confounded our firstborn as he tried to decide the path forward.

My strong belief in how things should be made it difficult for my son to embrace what is. His love for science was all about knowledge and sharing that knowledge with others. A flashback to second grade reminded me of this truth. While reading science books in school, Christopher would get in trouble for talking in class. "Did you know the vampire bat doesn't suck blood—it licks it?" he would say to anyone in earshot. He was a natural teacher. He just didn't know it—yet.

Letting go of your kids is more like a dance and less like a white-flag surrender. You can re-engage when necessary as long as your partner is willing. My suggestion to try on teaching didn't fall flat. "I could be a great science teacher," Christopher said. "I want kids to love science like I do."

That was the moment a teacher was born.

The struggle over what he didn't want to do was his alone. I'm grateful that when he punched through to the other side, I was there to witness it. Being a witness to his growing up is more satisfying than doing it for him.

THOUGHT POKE

It's so tempting to jump in and make decisions for your kids when they are struggling to decide. But their growth comes in that struggle. How can you be their lifeline to call when they need advice—instead of being their life?

> The path of the righteous is like the
> morning sun,
> shining ever brighter till the full
> light of day. (Prov. 4:18)

WHEN THE LEADER LETS GO

Train up a child in the way he should go, and
when he is old he will not depart from it.

Proverbs 22:6 (NKJV)

Do you remember teaching your child how to ride a bike? I do. It was a harrowing experience for both me and my firstborn. We started the process in the usual way: first the tricycle, then the big-boy bike with training wheels, and then finally taking off the training wheels and running alongside the wobbly and not yet confident boy. Christopher had two things working against him. He wasn't all that coordinated, and we lived on a very busy street, which made practicing a rare occurrence.

There are rules of the road for bike riders. They need to ride with traffic and not against it. They need to wear a helmet. They need working brakes. They need to use hand signals when they turn to let those with whom they share the road know where they are going. They need either a light or reflectors on their bikes so they can be seen at night. They're not supposed to ride on the sidewalk!

There's doctrine for being a safe bike rider that outlines specifically what you can and can't do. The rules of the road were true when teaching Christopher how to ride a bike, and they were true when teaching him how to drive. These rules need to be followed, whether or not Mom and Dad are running beside you.

We start them out on training wheels and then transition to running alongside them while their helmets are on and their elbows and knees are covered. Then we just let go—often without telling them we did so—and watch them pedal forward under their own power.

Knowing I have communicated doctrine well is the only way I can let go without losing control. We can supervise from a distance when we know our kids have learned the rules of the road.

THOUGHT POKE

How well have you communicated the doctrine of your family, of your faith? Remember that it is easier to let go when your kids know the way home.

> I trust in you, LORD;
> I say, "You are my God."
> (Ps. 31:14)

Day 52

THE GRASS IS
ALWAYS GREENER

Start where you are. Distant fields always look
greener, but opportunity lies right where you are.
Take advantage of every opportunity of service.
Robert Collier, *Riches within Your Reach!*

The comparisons began the moment you brought your
newborn home from the hospital (or out of your bedroom, as the case may be). How soon did your baby sleep
through the night? When did he sit up unaided? When

did she let go of your hand and walk? Where is he on the growth chart? Is she able to feed herself? When your best friend's little one went down the slide on his own while yours still sat in your lap, you started to wonder if the grass is indeed greener on the other side of the playground.

The parents you were surrounded by when your child was born may be the parents you're still surrounded by today. Only now the comparisons have morphed into identity-shattering witnesses of what you've done right (or not so right) as a parent. I admit that I watched in awe (and with some self-loathing) as a friend with five children launched all five successfully and "on time." They each graduated with honors, are financially independent, and are leaders in their communities. No one got into trouble. No one took second place—in anything. No one had trouble paying his phone bill. I have two children. Only two. Yet our younger son called just the other day, asking for thirty dollars for gas. It makes me question whether I let go too soon or held on too long.

Tending to a green lawn takes a lot of effort—and expense. So many factors contribute to its greenness. I've lived in a place where we were in a perpetual drought even though we were surrounded by water on three sides. I've lived in an arid climate where from above all you saw was the cracked, parched earth below. And I've lived in a place where the grass is green and no one ever waters it. I also watch a lot of home-improvement television shows, and some experts are now beginning to recommend artificial turf instead of a real lawn—maintenance free and always green. I think when we wonder if the grass is greener on the other side—in someone else's life, with someone else's kids—we need to consider the environment in which it grows.

So my son needs thirty dollars for gas this week. Does that mean we've failed? Does it mean he's not ready to be on his own? Or does it mean he's going through a difficult time and during this time we can still be the safety net he needs as he climbs up and away from us? I'd like to believe it's the latter. He's trying to bloom where he's planted but in a hostile environment. It's still possible—he just needs more water and added nutrients than other plants in order to thrive.

Each environment has its own opportunities for growth. Desert plants are just as beautiful as tropical ones.

Each climate zone has its own requirements for optimal growth and production. I've learned that my family doesn't live in the same zone as many of my friends. That means I need to be careful when making comparisons. After all, it's not recommended to plant a cactus in the rain forest, nor is it smart to try to cultivate a banana tree in the desert. And if you see such a thing, remember that it's probably an artificial plant anyway.

THOUGHT POKE

It may be tempting to look to the right and to the left and see a better place to raise your children. But be encouraged that you and they can bloom where planted. Look for ways to make the best of the situation in which God has placed you. Add nutrients where needed, but rest assured that your children can bloom.

> Each person should remain in the situation they were in when God called them.
> Were you a slave when you were called? Don't let it trouble you—although

if you can gain your freedom, do so. For the one who was a slave when called to faith in the Lord is the Lord's freed person; similarly, the one who was free when called is Christ's slave. You were bought at a price; do not become slaves of human beings. Brothers and sisters, each person, as responsible to God, should remain in the situation they were in when God called them. (1 Cor. 7:20–24)

BIBLE CREDITS